THE EVERYTHING DOG
ORGANIZER

THE ESSENTIAL PET RECORD KEEPER
AND DOG-CARE HANDBOOK

City
Dog

ISBN 1-933068-44-2

Design: Carol Salvin
Cover Illustration: Bill Kheel

Editor: Cricky Long
Associate Editor: Bryce Longton
Production Coordinator: Michelle Reiser
Copy Editor: Cristina Markarian

City Dog Publishing
P.O. Box 69636
West Hollywood, CA 90069
www.citydog.net

Printed in Thailand

DISCLAIMER

The purpose of this book is to inform and to entertain. Every effort was made to ensure that all information contained in this book was accurate and up-to-date at the time of publication. However, the authors, editor and City Dog Publishing, LLC shall have neither liability nor responsibility to any person or entity with respect to any loss or damage caused, or alleged to have been caused, directly or indirectly, by the information contained in this book. **IF YOUR DOG REQUIRES MEDICAL ATTENTION, CONTACT YOUR VET OR ANIMAL EMERGENCY FACILITY IMMEDIATELY.**

city dog wants to hear from you!

The Everything Dog Organizer is intended for use by anyone with a dog in their life. Whether you are prepping your home for a new puppy or just need to add a little organization to your household, this organizer is designed to make your life easier and your dog's life better. We hope you find it to be user-friendly and chock-full of helpful dog information. However, if you find that certain sections could be improved upon, please let us know. We would also love to know which parts of this book you found to be particularly helpful.

To learn more about other City Dog organizational accessories, visit our website at citydog.net.

Thank you!
The City Dog Team

Comments, questions and requests can be made online at citydog.net or by e-mailing, calling or faxing us.

City Dog Publishing
(866) 997-36477 (phone)
publisher@citydog.net

NAME . . . .

DATE OF BIRTH . . . .

☐ FEMALE   ☐ MALE

BREED(S) . . . .

. . . .

FUR COLOR(S) . . . .

. . . .

MARKINGS . . . .

SIZE . . . .

WEIGHT . . . .

MEDICATION . . . .

DOSAGE/FREQUENCY . . . .

GIVE WITH . . . .

MEDICATION . . . .

DOSAGE/FREQUENCY . . . .

GIVE WITH . . . .

ALLERGIES . . . .

. . . .

. . . .

PICTURE

eating

I eat . . . . cup(s)/can(s) of . . . .

. . . .

Special preparation . . . .

. . . .

My food is kept . . . .

. . . .

☑ I uaually eat breakfast at *7:30 – 8:00 am*

☑ I usually eat dinner at *5:00 p.m.*

☐ I eat once a day at . . . .

☐ I do **not** like to be touched while eating

My treats are kept . . . .

. . . .

☐ I am allowed to have . . . . treats a day

☐ No treats for me—I am
  ☐ on a diet
  ☐ allergic

I ☑ **am** ☐ **am not** allowed to eat table scraps
  ☐ Except ☑ Only *chicken, carrots* *Tiny amts of*

walking

My leash is kept . . . .

. . . .

My baggies are kept . . . .

. . . .

I am usually walked . . . . . times a day
(circle/check all times that apply)

AM	5	6	7	8	9	10	11							
PM	12	1	2	3	4	5	6	7	8	9	10	11		

  ☐ Whenever you wake up
  ☐ After meals
  ☐ After naps
  ☐ Each time you enter the house
  ☐ Before you go to bed

My idea of the perfect walk is
  ☐ A quick potty break
  ☐ A slow stroll
  ☐ A run

attitude

I may have an issue with
  ☐ Big dogs
  ☐ Small dogs
  ☐ All dogs
  ☐ Certain dogs . . . .
  ☐ Visitors
  ☐ Mailmen/delivery men
  ☐ Children
  ☐ Cats
  ☐ Separation anxiety

When backed into a corner, I am more likely to
  ☐ Go down fighting
  ☐ Roll over and play dead
  ☐ Other . . . .

Given the opportunity, I will
  ☑ Smother you with kisses
  ☐ Bite your finger off
  ☐ Escape
  ☐ Other . . . .

My bark ☐ **is** ☐ **is not** worse than my bite

dog owner 1

Name _Kathy andrew_

Home Phone _(925) 240 — 0290_

Work Phone _(   )   —_

Cell Phone _(925) 437 — 4349_

E-mail _KathyAndrew@ sbcglobal.net_

Other _____

Address _____

City, State, ZIP _____

dog owner 2

Name _manuel andrew_

Home Phone _(←)   —_

Work Phone _(925) 240 — 0160_

Cell Phone _(925) 980 — 7992_

E-mail _____

☐ Same Address

Address _____

City, State, ZIP _____

Notes

helpful people

NEIGHBORS, FAMILY MEMBERS OR CLOSE FRIENDS WHO WILL SHOW UP IN AN EMERGENCY

Name NancyNisBott (sis)

Home Phone (925) 778 — 9738

Work Phone ( ) —

Cell Phone ( ) —

E-mail

Notes

(son) simpkins

Name Greg + Sherry

Home Phone (925) 305 — 6436

Work Phone ( ) —

Cell Phone (925) 305 — 6436

E-mail

Notes ↑ son

Name

Home Phone ( ) —

Work Phone ( ) —

Cell Phone ( ) —

E-mail

Notes

Name

Home Phone ( ) —

Work Phone ( ) —

Cell Phone ( ) —

E-mail

Notes

emergency care   SEE NEXT PG. FOR REG. Vet.

> See the **CRITICAL CONDITIONS** section for information on life-threatening conditions and ailments.

24-HOUR/AFTER-HOURS EMERGENCY FACILITY
Business card in plastic pocket ☐ Yes ☐ No

Facility Name East Bay Vet ER

Phone (925) 754- — 5001

Address 1312 Sunset Dr.

Cross St. Hillcrest

City, State, ZIP Antioch, Ca

Office Hours

m - thursday
Weekdays 6 p.m. till 8:00 a.m.
Fri + weekends + Holidays.
Weekends 6 p.m. Fri. + then
24 Hours on weekend + Holidays

24/7   ☐ Yes ☐ No

Exam Fee $

Payment methods
☐ Check ✓ Credit cards ☐ Other

Notes call me for c.c. info

ANIMAL AMBULANCE
Business card in plastic pocket ☐ Yes ☐ No

Business Name

Phone (...) —

Service Hours

Weekdays

Weekends
24/7   ☐ Yes ☐ No

Emergency Transport Fee $

Payment methods
☐ Check ☐ Credit cards ☐ Other

Notes

veterinarian

WHAT TO LOOK FOR IN A VET

The best way to find a good vet is to survey in-the-know dog-o-philes—groomers, pet sitters, day-care owners, dog trainers, pet-supply-shop owners and people at the dog park. When you start to hear the same name over and over again, you have probably found a vet worth considering.

QUESTIONS TO ASK DOG-O-PHILES IN YOUR VET QUEST

- In what context do you know the vet? (Is your dog a patient or do you know the vet professionally?)

- How difficult is it to get an appointment?

- How accommodating is the office of last-minute appointments and emergencies?

- What is the vet's bedside manner like?

- How does the support staff treat you and your dog?

- What do you like best about the vet or practice?

While you'll never be certain you've found the right vet until you meet her, you can certainly do a preliminary screening by calling the vet's office and speaking to the support staff.

QUESTIONS TO ASK A POTENTIAL VETERINARY CLINIC OR OFFICE

- What is the cost of a routine exam?

- What are the vet's credentials?

- How many years of experience does the vet have?

- How many years has the practice been in business?

- Will your dog see the same vet each time or will he be relegated to whoever is available on the day you come in?

- Are there any specialists (cardiologists, oncologists, orthopedic surgeons, etc.) on staff?

- Does the practice offer any alternative treatment options, such as acupuncture, chiropractics or herbal therapies?

- What 24-hour or after-hours emergency facility does the vet refer patients to?

See **INFO SHEETS** section for **Vet Instruction Forms**.

Notes . . . .

. . . .

. . . .

. . . .

primary vet

Business card in plastic pocket ☐ Yes ☐ No

Facility Name Bishop Ranch

Veterinarian Frank utchen

Specialty

Phone (925) 966 — 8387

Address 2000 Bishop Drive at Norris Canyon Rd

Cross St. Norris Canyon

City, State, ZIP San Ramon Ca 94583

Website www.webvets.com

Other vets in practice (in order of preference)

1. DR. Kerr

2. Dr. Pogrel

Office Hours

Weekdays Mon- Friday 7:00 am to 12 midnight

☐ Closed for lunch

Saturdays 8am - 8 p.m

Sundays 8am - 8 p.m

24/7 ☐ Yes ☐ No

Exam Fee $

Payment methods
☐ Check ☑ Credit Cards ☐ Other

additional vet 1

Business card in plastic pocket ☐ Yes ☐ No

Facility Name

Veterinarian

Specialty

Phone ( ) —

Address

Cross St.

City, State, ZIP

Website

Other vets in practice (in order of preference)

1.

2.

Office Hours

Weekdays

☐ Closed for lunch

Saturdays

Sundays

24/7 ☐ Yes ☐ No

Exam Fee $

Payment methods
☐ Check ☐ Credit Cards ☐ Other

additional vet 2

Business card in plastic pocket ☐ Yes ☐ No

Facility Name . . . .

Veterinarian . . . .

Specialty . . . .

Phone (. . . .) . . . . — . . . .

Address . . . .

Cross St. . . . .

City, State, ZIP . . . .

Website . . . .

Other vets in practice (in order of preference)

1 . . . .

2 . . . .

Office Hours

  Weekdays . . . .

  ☐ Closed for lunch . . . .

  Saturdays . . . .

  Sundays . . . .

  24/7 ☐ Yes ☐ No

Exam Fee $ . . . .

Payment methods
  ☐ Check ☐ Credit Cards ☐ Other . . . . .

Notes . . . .

. . . .

. . . .

. . . .

. . . .

. . . .

. . . .

. . . .

. . . .

. . . .

. . . .

. . . .

. . . .

. . . .

. . . .

. . . .

. . . .

. . . .

. . . .

vaccination log

DATE	VACCINATION	EXPIRES	NOTES

medical/dental log

Date . . . .

Vet/technician . . . .

Reason for visit . . . .

. . . .

Diagnosis . . . .

. . . .

Treatment . . . .

. . . .

Follow-up . . . .

. . . .

Medication . . . .

. . . .

. . . .

Date . . . .

Vet/technician . . . .

Reason for visit . . . .

. . . .

Diagnosis . . . .

. . . .

Treatment . . . .

. . . .

Follow-up . . . .

. . . .

Medication . . . .

. . . .

. . . .

Notes . . . .

. . . .

. . . .

. . . .

. . . .

Notes . . . .

. . . .

. . . .

. . . .

. . . .

Date . . . .

Vet/technician . . . .

Reason for visit . . . .

. . . .

Diagnosis . . . .

. . . .

Treatment . . . .

. . . .

Follow-up . . . .

. . . .

Medication . . . .

. . . .

. . . .

Notes . . . .

. . . .

. . . .

. . . .

. . . .

. . . .

Date . . . .

Vet/technician . . . .

Reason for visit . . . .

. . . .

Diagnosis . . . .

. . . .

Treatment . . . .

. . . .

Follow-up . . . .

. . . .

Medication . . . .

. . . .

. . . .

Notes . . . .

. . . .

. . . .

. . . .

. . . .

. . . .

Date . . . .

Vet/technician . . . .

Reason for visit . . . .

. . . .

Diagnosis . . . .

. . . .

Treatment . . . .

. . . .

Follow-up . . . .

. . . .

Medication . . . .

. . . .

. . . .

Date . . . .

Vet/technician . . . .

Reason for visit . . . .

. . . .

Diagnosis . . . .

. . . .

Treatment . . . .

. . . .

Follow-up . . . .

. . . .

Medication . . . .

. . . .

. . . .

Notes . . . .

. . . .

. . . .

. . . .

. . . .

. . . .

Notes . . . .

. . . .

. . . .

. . . .

. . . .

. . . .

Date . . . .

Vet/technician . . . .

Reason for visit . . . .

. . . .

Diagnosis . . . .

. . . .

Treatment . . . .

. . . .

Follow-up . . . .

. . . .

Medication . . . .

. . . .

. . . .

Notes . . . .

. . . .

. . . .

. . . .

. . . .

. . . .

Date . . . .

Vet/technician . . . .

Reason for visit . . . .

. . . .

Diagnosis . . . .

. . . .

Treatment . . . .

. . . .

Follow-up . . . .

. . . .

Medication . . . .

. . . .

Notes . . . .

. . . .

. . . .

. . . .

. . . .

. . . .

Date . . . .

Vet/technician . . . .

Reason for visit . . . .

. . . .

Diagnosis . . . .

. . . .

Treatment . . . .

. . . .

Follow-up . . . .

. . . .

Medication . . . .

. . . .

. . . .

Date . . . .

Vet/technician . . . .

Reason for visit . . . .

. . . .

Diagnosis . . . .

. . . .

Treatment . . . .

. . . .

Follow-up . . . .

. . . .

Medication . . . .

. . . .

. . . .

Notes . . . .

. . . .

. . . .

. . . .

. . . .

. . . .

Notes . . . .

. . . .

. . . .

. . . .

. . . .

. . . .

Date . . . .

Vet/technician . . . .

Reason for visit . . . .

. . . .

Diagnosis . . . .

. . . .

Treatment . . . .

. . . .

Follow-up . . . .

. . . .

Medication . . . .

. . . .

. . . .

Date . . . .

Vet/technician . . . .

Reason for visit . . . .

. . . .

Diagnosis . . . .

. . . .

Treatment . . . .

. . . .

Follow-up . . . .

. . . .

Medication . . . .

. . . .

. . . .

Notes . . . .

Notes . . . .

Dog Vitals | MEDICAL/DENTAL LOG

Date . . . .

Vet/technician . . . .

Reason for visit . . . .

. . . .

Diagnosis . . . .

. . . .

Treatment . . . .

. . . .

Follow-up . . . .

. . . .

Medication . . . .

. . . .

. . . .

Date . . . .

Vet/technician . . . .

Reason for visit . . . .

. . . .

Diagnosis . . . .

. . . .

Treatment . . . .

. . . .

Follow-up . . . .

. . . .

Medication . . . .

. . . .

. . . .

Notes . . . .

. . . .

. . . .

. . . .

. . . .

. . . .

Notes . . . .

. . . .

. . . .

. . . .

. . . .

. . . .

Date . . . .

Vet/technician . . . .

Reason for visit . . . .

. . . .

Diagnosis . . . .

. . . .

Treatment . . . .

. . . .

Follow-up . . . .

. . . .

Medication . . . .

. . . .

. . . .

Notes . . . .

. . . .

. . . .

. . . .

. . . .

. . . .

Date . . . .

Vet/technician . . . .

Reason for visit . . . .

. . . .

Diagnosis . . . .

. . . .

Treatment . . . .

. . . .

Follow-up . . . .

. . . .

Medication . . . .

. . . .

Notes . . . .

. . . .

. . . .

. . . .

. . . .

. . . .

Dog Vitals | MEDICAL/DENTAL LOG

Date . . . .

Vet/technician . . . .

Reason for visit . . . .

. . . .

Diagnosis . . . .

. . . .

Treatment . . . .

. . . .

Follow-up . . . .

. . . .

Medication . . . .

. . . .

. . . .

Date . . . .

Vet/technician . . . .

Reason for visit . . . .

. . . .

Diagnosis . . . .

. . . .

Treatment . . . .

. . . .

Follow-up . . . .

. . . .

Medication . . . .

. . . .

. . . .

Notes . . . .

. . . .

. . . .

. . . .

. . . .

. . . .

Notes . . . .

. . . .

. . . .

. . . .

. . . .

. . . .

411

Date . . . .

Vet/technician . . . .

Reason for visit . . . .

. . . .

Diagnosis . . . .

. . . .

Treatment . . . .

. . . .

Follow-up . . . .

. . . .

Medication . . . .

. . . .

. . . .

Notes . . . .

. . . .

. . . .

. . . .

. . . .

. . . .

Date . . . .

Vet/technician . . . .

Reason for visit . . . .

. . . .

Diagnosis . . . .

. . . .

Treatment . . . .

. . . .

Follow-up . . . .

. . . .

Medication . . . .

. . . .

. . . .

Notes . . . .

. . . .

. . . .

. . . .

. . . .

. . . .

411

pet-supply stores

Store 1 . . . .

Business card in plastic pocket ☐ Yes ☐ No

Phone (. . . .) . . . . — . . . .

Address . . . .

Cross St. . . . .

City, State , ZIP . . . .

. . . .

Hours

Weekdays . . . .

Saturday . . . .

Sunday . . . .

Payment methods
☐ Check ☐ Credit cards ☐ Other . . . . .

Owner/Manager(s) . . . .

. . . .

Dog Food(s) . . . .

. . . .

Treat(s) . . . .

. . . .

Rawhide . . . .

Supplement(s) . . . .

. . . .

Flea-Prevention Treatment . . . .

. . . .

Miscellaneous Product(s) . . . .

. . . .

. . . .

Foods/Products to Avoid . . . .

. . . .

. . . .

Services Offered . . . .

. . . .

. . . .

Parking/Delivery Options . . . .

. . . .

Notes . . . .

. . . .

. . . .

Store 2 . . . .

Business card in plastic pocket ☐ Yes ☐ No

Phone   (. . . .) . . . . — . . . .

Address . . . .

Cross St. . . . .

City, State , ZIP . . . .

Hours

   Weekdays . . . .

   Saturday . . . .

   Sunday . . . .

Payment methods
   ☐ Check ☐ Credit cards ☐ Other . . . . .

Owner/Manager(s) . . . .

Dog Food(s) . . . .

Treat(s) . . . .

Rawhide . . . .

Supplement(s) . . . .

Flea-Prevention Treatment . . . .

Miscellaneous Product(s) . . . .

Foods/Products to Avoid . . . .

Services Offered . . . .

Parking/Delivery Options . . . .

Notes

dog walker/pet sitter

WHAT TO LOOK FOR IN A PET SITTER When you are looking for a sitter,* think about whether you want to go with a large pet sitting/dog-walking company or with an individual. One is not necessarily better than the other. It really comes down to personal preference.

INDIVIDUAL PET SITTER

PROS

- Your dog gets the same sitter each visit
- It feels more personal than a pet sitting company
- You know who has the key to your home

CONS

- Unless your sitter has a committed backup, there is no one to fill in in an emergency
- You are relying on one person's availability

QUESTIONS TO ASK

- Is pet sitting this person's full-time job or is this a part-time job? (Part-time sitters often have a harder time accommodating your schedule)
- How long has this person been working as a pet sitter?
- Does this person have any formal animal-care training?

BIG-BUSINESS PET SITTING COMPANY

PROS

- Someone will be able to fill in if your regular pet sitter suddenly can't make it
- The company screens employees for you, some even do background checks
- Employees are usually required to attend some sort of training program or session

CONS

- It lacks the personal connection found with an individual sitter
- Your dog may not get the same sitter each visit
- "Company policy" can translate into more surcharges and less flexibility

QUESTIONS TO ASK

- What sort of screening process does the company use when hiring employees?
- How does the company train its employees?
- How long has the company been in business?
- Will the same pet sitter visit your dog each time?

5 **SUREFIRE WAYS TO DRIVE YOUR PET SITTER CRAZY**

1. Leave the alarm on without giving him the code. Or even better, give him the code, then change it without telling him.
2. Wait until the last possible moment to cancel his visit.
3. Hide leashes and baggies.
4. Never pay on time.
5. Leave him lots of illegible notes.

THE PET SITTER CONSULTATION   This initial meet-and-greet gives you the opportunity to ask the dog walker/pet sitter questions while she assesses your needs and meets your dog.

QUESTIONS TO ASK A POTENTIAL SITTER
- Is the sitter a member of Pet Sitters International (PSI) or a similar organization?
- Is the sitter bonded and insured?
- Is the sitter certified in pet first-aid and CPR?
- Does the sitter take dogs on solo or group walks? If group walks:
  - What is the maximum number of dogs he will take out at a time?
  - What does he do with your dog while collecting other dogs from their homes?
  - How are the dogs screened and introduced to one another?
- Does the sitter take dogs to off-leash parks? If yes, are the parks fenced-in?
- Will the sitter reinforce obedience training with your dog?
- Does the sitter work evenings/weekends/holidays?
- Can the sitter accommodate last-minute appointments?
- Does the sitter do any other household chores? (e.g., closing/opening blinds, taking out the trash, feeding other animals, cleaning the litter box, collecting the mail)
- Will the sitter spend the night at your house? If yes, what time does he arrive and what time does he leave in the morning?

- Will the sitter administer medication?

> *Most pet sitters will give medications in pill form. If your pet requires injections, you should consider hiring a pet sitter who has been trained as a vet tech.*

- Has the sitter ever had to deal with an emergency while pet sitting? If yes, how did he resolve the situation?
- Does the sitter have a vet on call in the event of an emergency?
- What procedures does the sitter follow in the event of an emergency?
- Does the sitter offer discount packages?

> *Your pet sitter should provide you with a list of rates and fees as well as a pet sitting contract.*

- Does the sitter charge premiums for any services?
- Will the sitter supply you with references? (Always check references!)

> See **INFO SHEETS** section for **Pet Sitter Instruction Forms**.

*The term "sitter" applies to both individuals and pet sitting companies and includes both pet sitters and dog walkers.

pet sitter contact sheet

Pet Sitter 1 margaret Dillon
Business card in plastic pocket ☐Yes ☐No

Phone (415) 664 - 0699

Cell/Pager (415) 810 - 0881

E-mail md2713@sbc.com

work
~~Website~~ 415 - 542 - 3579

Weekdays Hours . . . . Rate . . . .

Weekend Hours . . . . Rate . . . .

Holiday Hours . . . . Rate . . . .

Overnights . . . . Rate . . . .

Pet Sitter 2 . . . .
Business card in plastic pocket ☐Yes ☐No

Phone (. . .) —

Cell/Pager (. . .) —

E-mail . . . .

Website . . . .

Weekdays Hours . . . . Rate . . . .

Weekend Hours . . . . Rate . . . .

Holiday Hours . . . . Rate . . . .

Overnights . . . . Rate . . . .

Pet Sitter 3 . . . .
Business card in plastic pocket ☐Yes ☐No

Phone (. . .) —

Cell/Pager (. . .) —

E-mail . . . .

Website . . . .

Weekdays Hours . . . . Rate . . . .

Weekend Hours . . . . Rate . . . .

Holiday Hours . . . . Rate . . . .

Overnights . . . . Rate . . . .

Pet Sitter 4 . . . .
Business card in plastic pocket ☐Yes ☐No

Phone (. . .) —

Cell/Pager (. . .) —

E-mail . . . .

Website . . . .

Weekdays Hours . . . . Rate . . . .

Weekend Hours . . . . Rate . . . .

Holiday Hours . . . . Rate . . . .

Overnights . . . . Rate . . . .

day care/boarding

THE DAY CARE INTERVIEW   While some people claim it's easier to get accepted into an Ivy League college than to survive the rigorous dog-day-care interview, the purpose of this interview is to weed out antisocial dogs and make sure your dog is current on his shots.

QUESTIONS TO ASK DURING THE INTERVIEW

DAY CARE

- What is the staff/dog ratio?
- What sort of training has the staff had?
- What is the maximum number of dogs the facility will accept at one time?

> *There is no magic number of dogs or staff members that will ensure a safe environment for your dog. However, the closer the staff/dog ratio, the better.*

- Are dogs supervised at all times?
- Are small, timid and/or elderly dogs separated from larger and/or more rambunctious pups?
- Is there a screening process to weed out aggressive or antisocial dogs?
- What does the staff do in the event of a dogfight?
- Is there a vet on call in the event of an emergency, or if your dog gets sick?
- How often do the dogs get to go outside?
- Are there designated potty areas, or does the facility have more of a pee-where-you-please mentality?
- Do dogs have access to water at all times?
- Are dogs ever taken on walks? If so, how many times a day and for how long?
- Do dogs have a place to go to escape the sun or cold?

- Is there bedding or a nap area?
- Does the facility provide food or treats? If so, what kind? If not, can you bring your own?

BOARDING

- Does the facility offer overnight care?
- Is there someone onsite at all times?
- Can you bring your pup's bedding from home?
- Are dogs ever crated? If so, when?
- If dogs stay in individual runs, how often are they walked or taken out to play in a larger run?
- Does the facility permit group play? (Under what circumstances?)
- What happens if you are late to pick up your dog?
- What vaccinations does the facility require?
- Will the facility provide you with references? (Always check references.)

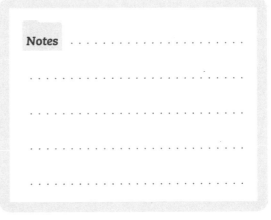

Notes . . . .

. . . .

. . . .

. . . .

. . . .

day care/boarding contact sheet

Facility 1 . . . .
Business card in plastic pocket ☐Yes ☐No

Phone   (. . . .) . . . . . . — . . . .

Address . . . .

Cross St. . . . .

City, State, ZIP . . . .

Office Hours

  Weekdays . . . .

    ☐ Closed for lunch . . . .

  Saturdays . . . .

  Sundays . . . .
24/7   ☐Yes ☐No

Day Care Fee $ . . . .

Boarding Fee $ . . . .

Payment methods
  ☐Check ☐Credit cards ☐Other . . . . .

Facility 2 . . . .
Business card in plastic pocket ☐Yes ☐No

Phone   (. . . .) . . . . . . — . . . .

Address . . . .

Cross St. . . . .

City, State, ZIP . . . .

Office Hours

  Weekdays . . . .

    ☐ Closed for lunch . . . .

  Saturdays . . . .

  Sundays . . . .
24/7   ☐Yes ☐No

Day Care Fee $ . . . .

Boarding Fee $ . . . .

Payment methods
  ☐Check ☐Credit cards ☐Other . . . . .

5 SUREFIRE WAYS TO DRIVE THE STAFF OF YOUR DOG'S DAY CARE CRAZY

1. Regularly pick up your dog late, it'll give the staff extra time to bond with him.
2. Bring your dog to day care when he's sick. The other dogs will make him feel better.
3. Don't worry if your dog has fleas. If all the other dogs are on flea-prevention treatment like they're supposed to be, it shouldn't be an issue.
4. Call regularly and ask to speak to your dog. It's important for your pup to hear your voice throughout the day.
5. Make as many unusual requests as possible. After all, your dog deserves special treatment.

411

Facility 3

Business card in plastic pocket ☐ Yes ☐ No

Phone (. . .) . . . . . . — . . . .

Address . . . .

Cross St. . . . .

City, State, ZIP . . . .

Office Hours

  Weekdays . . . .

    ☐ Closed for lunch . . . .

  Saturdays . . . .

  Sundays . . . .

  24/7 ☐ Yes ☐ No

Day Care Fee $ . . . .

Boarding Fee $ . . . .

Payment methods

  ☐ Check ☐ Credit cards ☐ Other . . . .

Facility 4

Business card in plastic pocket ☐ Yes ☐ No

Phone (. . .) . . . . . . — . . . .

Address . . . .

Cross St. . . . .

City, State, ZIP . . . .

Office Hours

  Weekdays . . . .

    ☐ Closed for lunch . . . .

  Saturdays . . . .

  Sundays . . . .

  24/7 ☐ Yes ☐ No

Day Care Fee $ . . . .

Boarding Fee $ . . . .

Payment methods

  ☐ Check ☐ Credit cards ☐ Other . . . .

Notes . . . .

. . . .

. . . .

. . . .

. . . .

groomers

Unless you're willing to endure the bending-over-the-tub back pain that comes with bathing your dog, you'll need to find a good groomer. By relegating your dog-washing duties to a professional, you also get to skip the following hygienic procedures, which usually come standard with full-service grooming: nail clipping, ear cleaning, anal-gland expression and trimming fur around the paws.

Many grooming salons also offer optional amenities such as anesthesia-free teeth cleaning, nail painting and spa services like hot oil treatments, dog massage and aroma-therapy.

QUESTIONS TO ASK AND THINGS TO CONSIDER WHEN CHOOSING A GROOMER

- How long has the salon been in business?
- What is the general atmosphere in the salon?
  - How do the groomers and staff treat the dogs?
  - Are dogs groomed assembly line-style or do groomers provide personalized service?
  - Is it clean?
- How much experience does the groomer have?
- Is the groomer certified as a master groomer?
  Note: Certified master groomers undergo extensive training to groom dogs per the breed standard. If you're looking for a casual pet clip for your mixed-breed dog, it is not necessary to find a master groomer.
- What methods does the groomer use—hand scissoring or clipping?
  Note: Hand scissoring requires more skill and takes longer, but the end result is much more polished.
- Does the groomer offer hand stripping?
  Note: This is important if you have a terrier. Hand stripping is a process that pulls

Notes . . . .

dead hair out of wire-haired breeds, providing a flatter, more waterproof, less matted coat for the dog. Hand stripping is what gives these breeds their standard look.

- How are the dogs dried? By hand? Cage? Fan?
  Important Note: When used improperly, a heated cage dryer can cause heat stroke and kill a dog in a matter of minutes. If your groomer uses cage dryers, make sure the dryers are temperature-controlled and that dogs are supervised at all times during the drying process.

- What types of shampoos are used?
  - Does the salon offer medicated shampoos for dogs with fleas, itchy skin or hot spots?
  - Does the salon offer hypoallergenic shampoos for dogs with sensitive skin?
  - Can you bring your own shampoo?

- What are the drop-off/pickup hours?
  - Some shops have a first-come, first-served policy. If you have an old or large dog who is more likely to be cramped in one of the crates, drop off your dog as early as possible so your dog will have a shorter wait time
  - Believe it or not, there are times people actually forget to pick up their dog before the salon closes. Ask the shop what happens in the event that they close before you show up

- How far in advance do you need to schedule an appointment?

mobile grooming

With the rise in popularity of this service, mobile grooming vans are becoming increasingly high-tech. They also tend to be clean and well run. Beyond the obvious perk of having your dog groomed in your driveway—namely convenience—there are numerous other advantages:

- Your dog gets more personal attention

- Your dog doesn't have to spend time cooped up in a crate—this is especially good for older and larger dogs who tend to get stiff or sore when confined to a cage

THINGS TO BE AWARE OF

- Many groomers require electric and water hookups, so unless you can supply them with access to both, check first to make sure they are self contained

- You pay for the convenience of having a groomer come to you. While most mobile groomers do not charge a travel fee, the cost is generally reflected in the grooming bill

groomers contact sheet

Groomer 1
Business card in plastic pocket ☐ Yes ☐ No

Phone (. . .) . . . . . — . . . . . .

Address

Cross St.

City, State, ZIP

Website

Weekdays Hours

Saturday Hours

Notes

Groomer 2
Business card in plastic pocket ☐ Yes ☐ No

Phone (. . .) . . . . . — . . . . . .

Address

Cross St.

City, State, ZIP

Website

Weekdays Hours

Saturday Hours

Notes

Groomer 3
Business card in plastic pocket ☐ Yes ☐ No

Phone (. . .) . . . . . — . . . . . .

Address

Cross St.

City, State, ZIP

Website

Weekdays Hours

Saturday Hours

Notes

Groomer 4
Business card in plastic pocket ☐ Yes ☐ No

Phone (. . .) . . . . . — . . . . . .

Address

Cross St.

City, State, ZIP

Website

Weekdays Hours

Saturday Hours

Notes

trainers

- How are the trainer's presentation skills?
  - She should be able to move seamlessly between addressing the group as a whole, demonstrating the lesson, and working one on one with the students
  - She should allow students plenty of practice time so any questions can be addressed before the end of each class
  - She should provide students with written materials to complement the lessons

- What is the trainer/student ratio?
  - There should not be so many people that the trainer is unable to observe and critique each student in the class
  - If a fight should break out between two of the dogs, the trainer should be able to intervene in a timely, effective manner

- How does the trainer treat the dogs?
  - The trainer should never be physically or verbally abusive to the dogs!

- How does the trainer interact with the people in her class?
  - You should feel comfortable working with your dog trainer

- How do you feel about her training methods and style?

A GOOD TRAINER IS...

- Someone who is certified by the Association of Pet Dog Trainers (APDT)

- Someone who has been professionally trained or has apprenticed with an established dog trainer

- Someone who you trust and respect

- Someone who attends seminars and ongoing educational courses

- Someone who does not permit aggressive dogs to attend her group classes

Notes . . . .

. . . .

. . . .

. . . .

. . . .

trainers contact sheet

Trainer 1 . . . .
Business card in plastic pocket ☐Yes ☐No

Phone (. . . .) . . . . ─ . . . . . .

Cell/Pager (. . . .) . . . . . ─ . . . .

Address . . . .

Cross St. . . . .

City, State, ZIP . . . .

E-mail . . . .

Website . . . .

Hourly Rate . . . .

Class Rate . . . .

Trainer 2 . . . .
Business card in plastic pocket ☐Yes ☐No

Phone (. . . .) . . . . ─ . . . . . .

Cell/Pager (. . . .) . . . . . ─ . . . .

Address . . . .

Cross St. . . . .

City, State, ZIP . . . .

E-mail . . . .

Website . . . .

Hourly Rate . . . .

Class Rate . . . .

Trainer 3 . . . .
Business card in plastic pocket ☐Yes ☐No

Phone (. . . .) . . . . ─ . . . . . .

Cell/Pager (. . . .) . . . . . ─ . . . .

Address . . . .

Cross St. . . . .

City, State, ZIP . . . .

E-mail . . . .

Website . . . .

Hourly Rate . . . .

Class Rate . . . .

Trainer 4 . . . .
Business card in plastic pocket ☐Yes ☐No

Phone (. . . .) . . . . ─ . . . . . .

Cell/Pager (. . . .) . . . . . ─ . . . .

Address . . . .

Cross St. . . . .

City, State, ZIP . . . .

E-mail . . . .

Website . . . .

Hourly Rate . . . .

Class Rate . . . .

household poisons

> **IF YOU SUSPECT THAT YOUR DOG HAS BEEN POISONED, CALL YOUR VET OR THE ASPCA ANIMAL POISON CONTROL CENTER IMMEDIATELY.**

You can reach the ASPCA Animal Poison Control Center at **(888) 426-4435.**

A veterinary toxicologist is on duty 24 hours a day, 365 days a year, to diagnose your pet and recommend the appropriate treatment.

The **$50** consultation fee includes unlimited follow-up phone calls and, at your request, they will also advise your veterinarian at no additional charge.

To have the consultation fee automatically added to your phone bill, call (900) 433-0000. Do **not** dial the 900 number for follow-up calls. Instead, call (888) 299-2973.

> *In no way is the information in this section meant to replace emergency and/or routine veterinary care. The content of this book is designed for informational purposes only.*
>
> **IF YOUR DOG REQUIRES MEDICAL ATTENTION, CONTACT YOUR VET OR ANIMAL EMERGENCY FACILITY IMMEDIATELY.**

FOLLOWING IS A LIST OF COMMON HOUSEHOLD PRODUCTS AND FOODS THAT ARE TOXIC TO YOUR DOG*

- Alcohol
- Ant & roach traps/spray
- Antifreeze
- Avocados
- Chocolate
- Cleaning products
- Coffee
- Flea foggers/bombs/powders
- Fruit pits and seeds
- Gardening fertilizer
- Garlic
- Grapes
- Ibuprofen
- Insecticide
- Lead
- Medications (human)
- Mold
- Mushrooms
- Mustard seeds
- Nicotine
- Macadamia nuts
- Onions and onion powder
- Raisins
- Rat poison
- Salt
- Tylenol
- Walnuts
- Zinc

* **DO NOT** assume that something is not toxic simply because it is not on this list.

bloat

POTENTIALLY FATAL YES

After cancer, bloat is the second leading killer of dogs.

PREVENTABLE SOMEWHAT

- Feed your dog two small meals a day (as opposed to one large one)
- Keep stress to a minimum
- Prevent your dog from eating or drinking too quickly
- Do not allow your dog to drink too much water immediately before or after eating
- Do not allow your dog to exercise immediately before or after eating
- Do not allow your dog to eat the following substances
  - Alfalfa
  - Brewer's yeast
  - Soybean products
  - Foods that produce gas
  - Dry foods that contain citric acid as a preservative (risk of bloat is increased when you wet this food) or fat among the first four ingredients

> Bloat is the result of an abnormal accumulation of air and/or fluid in the stomach. This condition is sometimes but not always accompanied by a twisting of the stomach. The bloated condition and/or twisting leads to obstruction of veins, low blood pressure, shock, damage to internal organs and often death.

TREATABLE YES

But it is **critical** that you get your dog to the vet immediately! A dog can die from bloat in as little as one to two hours following the onset of symptoms!

SIGNS OF BLOAT

- Anxiety
- Attempting unsuccessfully to vomit
- Bloated abdomen
- Coughing/gagging
- Drinking excessive amounts of water
- Salivating
- Hiding
- Inability to lie or sit down
- Licking the air
- Off-color gums (red, blue or white)
- Pacing
- Rapid panting
- Shallow breathing
- Standing with legs spread apart
- Weakness
- Whining

DOGS MOST LIKELY TO SUFFER FROM BLOAT

- Large/extra large dogs
- Dogs with deep chests
- Breeds
  - Great Danes
  - St. Bernards
  - Weimaraners
- Male dogs
- Underweight dogs
- Anxious dogs
- Older Dogs (ages 4 – 10)

frostbite

POTENTIALLY FATAL   NO
However, in severe cases, limbs may need to be amputated.

PREVENTABLE   YES
- Use socks or dog boots to cover cold paws
- Use a dog jacket or sweater for dogs with short hair or dogs not used to the cold
- Never leave your dog outdoors unattended in inclement weather

TREATABLE   YES
Warning: Once you warm up the affected area, it will sting, so be gentle and be aware that your dog may attempt to bite you.

- Heat the affected area with warm—**not hot**—water
- Gently pat dry the affected area (no rubbing)
- Put a Vaseline-based ointment on the area and then wrap your dog in a towel or blanket
- Get your dog to the vet ASAP. Advanced frostbite requires amputation, and any level of frostbite is prone to infection

WHAT NOT TO DO FOR FROSTBITE
- Do not massage the area, as this could loosen toxins within the tissue and cause further damage
- Do not apply snow or ice
- Do not submerge your dog completely in warm water—this could cause hypothermia
- Do not warm your dog up too fast—it can be painful

SIGNS OF FROSTBITE
- Blisters on the affected area
- Ice on body and limbs
- Shivering
- Skin that changes from very pale to a bright red when warmed and then eventually to black

DOGS MOST LIKELY TO GET FROSTBITE
- Dogs with short fur
- Dogs that are not acclimated to cold weather

BODY PARTS MOST SUSCEPTIBLE TO FROSTBITE
- Ear tips
- Face
- Paws pads
- Scrotum
- Tail

Notes . . . .
. . . .
. . . .
. . . .

heartworm

POTENTIALLY FATAL YES

If left untreated, heartworm can be deadly

PREVENTABLE YES

- An all-in-one topical treatment that prevents heartworm, fleas and ticks is available by prescription

- Tablets administered on a monthly basis are available by prescription

TREATABLE YES

- Ask your vet to test your dog for heartworm during his annual exam

- Treatment is by prescription only

SIGNS OF HEARTWORM

- Abnormal sounds from the heart and lungs

- Chronic cough

- Shortness of breath

- Weakness

DOGS MOST LIKELY TO SUFFER FROM HEARTWORM

All dogs are susceptible to heartworm. However, heartworm is most common in the Southeast, the Southwest, the Eastern seaboard and the Midwest, although there have been incidents in all 50 U.S. states and Canada.

HOW DOGS CATCH HEARTWORM

When an infected mosquito bites a dog, it transmits heartworm larvae that ultimately grow into worms. Female worms can reach over a foot in length.

> **IF YOUR DOG REQUIRES MEDICAL ATTENTION, CONTACT YOUR VET OR ANIMAL EMERGENCY FACILITY IMMEDIATELY.**

Notes . . . .

. . . .

. . . .

. . . .

. . . .

. . . .

. . . .

heat stroke

POTENTIALLY FATAL YES

PREVENTABLE YES

- Avoid exercising your dog in the heat—early in the morning and evening are usually best

- Make sure your dog always has plenty of water

- Watch that your dog does not get overly excited in the heat

- Never leave your dog alone inside the car. Even on mild days, the temperature inside a car can reach dangerous levels. Cracking the windows does not provide sufficient ventilation!

- Never leave your dog outside in the heat unattended

- Never leave your dog confined to a crate in the heat

SIGNS OF HEAT STROKE

- Dizziness
- Excessive panting
- Excessive salivating
- Exhaustion
- Fever of 104° and higher
- Glazed eyes
- Loss of balance
- Red or gray gums
- Shallow/labored/noisy breathing

TREATABLE YES

- Stop all activity

- Move your dog to the shade

- Soak, rinse or wet him with cool—**not cold**—water

- Place a wet towel on his face and neck

  Important note: Do not cover his body with a wet towel; this will prevent heat from escaping.

- Offer small amounts of room-temperature water

- Once you have quickly cooled him down, take him to a vet ASAP

DOGS MOST LIKELY TO GET HEAT STROKE

- Dogs that spend most of their time in an air-conditioned environment
- Dogs with heart conditions
- Dogs with respiratory conditions
- Larger dogs
- Older dogs
- Overweight dogs
- Puppies
- Short-nosed dogs

- Normal Body Temperature: 100.5° – 102.5°
- Moderate Heat Stroke: 103° – 104°
- Severe Heat Stroke: 105° and higher

DO NOT LEAVE YOUR DOG IN THE CAR UNATTENDED!

hypothermia

POTENTIALLY FATAL   YES

PREVENTABLE   YES

- Never leave your dog outdoors unattended in inclement weather

- Never leave your dog in the car unattended in inclement weather

- Snow and/or ice interferes with your dog's sense of smell, which affects his sense of direction. Keep him on a leash so he won't get lost

- Depending on the age and health of your dog and the severity of the weather, you may want to keep him indoors except for quick potty breaks

- If your dog has short hair, buy him a coat

- Make sure your dog's sleeping quarters are draft-free, and preferably off the floor

TREATABLE   YES

- Contact your vet ASAP for advice

- If your dog is already wet, immerse him in a lukewarm—**not** hot—bath

- If your dog is dry, apply the following under armpits and on stomach

  - Water bottle with warm—**not** hot—water. If you don't have a water bottle, a plastic soda bottle will work, but be sure to insulate the bottle with a blanket or towel so as not to burn your dog

  - Well-insulated heating pad set on warm—**not** hot

  - Hair dryer set on low, with warm—**not** hot—air. Use extreme caution so you don't burn your dog

- Use your body heat to warm your dog by wrapping yourself up in a blanket with him

- Give him four tablespoons of sugar dissolved in a pint of room-temperature water. You may also use honey or caro or maple syrup

SIGNS OF HYPOTHERMIA

- Apathy

- Coma

- Dilated pupils

- Low heart rate

- Shivering

- Slow breathing

- Weakness

DOGS MOST LIKELY TO GET HYPOTHERMIA

- Older dogs

- Puppies

- Short-haired dogs

- Sick dogs

- Normal Body Temperature: 100.5° – 102.5°

- Mild Hypothermia: 96° – 100°

- Moderate Hypothermia: 90° – 95°

- Severe Hypothermia: Below 90°

lyme disease

POTENTIALLY FATAL **NOT USUALLY**
However, it is debilitating.

PREVENTABLE **SOMEWHAT**

- Give your dog a full-body tick check after he has been in the woods or high grass

- Spray lawn with vet-approved tick killer

- Keep lawn mowed

- Use a flea- and tick-preventative treatment (collar, dip, bath)

- Vaccinate your dog against Lyme disease on an annual basis
  Important Note: This vaccine is **not** 100% effective, so you should continue with other measures

TREATABLE **YES**

- With timely treatment, most dogs make a full recovery with no permanent joint or nerve damage

- Your vet will most likely prescribe tetracycline

SIGNS OF LYME DISEASE

- Apathy

- Limping

- Loss of appetite

- Severe joint pain

- Swelling in nodes

- Temperature of 103°

It usually takes at least 24 hours for a tick to transmit Lyme Disease to a person or a dog. By doing a full-body tick check on yourself and your dog every time you return from a hike, you are seriously reducing your chances of catching this disease. For information on **how to remove a tick** *see* **TICKS** *on page 46.*

Notes . . . .

. . . .

. . . .

. . . .

. . . .

. . . .

pancreatitis

POTENTIALLY FATAL YES
Acute pancreatitis can be fatal. However, chronic pancreatitis is typically not fatal.

PREVENTABLE YES
- Feed your dog a low-fat diet
- Exercise your dog regularly
- Add a small amount of fiber to your dog's diet
- Make sure your dog can't get into the trash, especially around the holidays
- Make sure people aren't slipping your dog snacks during holiday festivities

TREATABLE YES
Speak to your vet before proceeding with any of the following treatments

- Withhold food for 24 to 36 hours, then offer bland foods in small amounts (noodles or rice)
- Talk to your vet about administering sub-cutaneous fluids to help with dehydration
- Administer medication to help prevent vomiting

If your dog isn't eating because he is suffering from pancreatitis, the last thing you should do is give him something fatty to jumpstart his appetite.

SIGNS OF PANCREATITIS
- Abdominal pain
- Depression
- Diarrhea
- Drinking excessive amounts of water
- Exhaustion
- Fever
- Labored breathing
- Refusal to drink water
- Refusal to eat
- Restlessness
- Vomiting
- Weight loss

DOGS MOST LIKELY TO SUFFER FROM PANCREATITIS
- Breeds
  - Cocker spaniels
  - Miniature poodles
  - Miniature schnauzers
  - Yorkshire terriers
  - Silky terriers
- Overweight dogs
- Dogs with diabetes
- Dogs over the age of six

THE FOLLOWING ITEMS HAVE BEEN KNOWN TO CAUSE PANCREATITIS
- Antacids
- Antibiotics
- Diuretics
- Insecticides
- Tylenol

IF YOUR DOG REQUIRES MEDICAL ATTENTION, CONTACT YOUR VET OR ANIMAL EMERGENCY FACILITY IMMEDIATELY.

rattlesnakes

POTENTIALLY FATAL   YES

PREVENTABLE   YES

- Leash up! Keeping your dog on a leash is the best way to prevent a rattlesnake bite

- Enroll your dog in a rattlesnake-aversion training course where he will learn to avoid the sight, sound and/or smell of a rattlesnake through negative association

- Keep an eye out around rocks and crevices

- Do not let your dog dig around under rocks and logs

- Do not walk through tall grass or underbrush

- Do not hike at dusk or dawn, when you are most likely to encounter rattlesnakes

TREATABLE   YES—but you **MUST** act quickly

- If possible, immobilize your dog (activity causes the venom to spread), and carry your dog to the car or arrange for someone to pick the two of you up

- Get your dog to an animal hospital that can administer the anti-venom ASAP

RATTLESNAKE ANTI-VENOM

NOT ALL ANIMAL HOSPITALS CARRY THE ANTI-VENOM. IT IS VERY EXPENSIVE AND HAS A SHORT SHELF LIFE. BE PROACTIVE. FIND OUT

- **WHICH VETS IN YOUR AREA CARRY THE ANTI-VENOM**
- **HOW MUCH THEY KEEP ON HAND**
- **HOW FREQUENTLY THEY RESTOCK THEIR SUPPLY.**

---

rocky mountain spotted fever

POTENTIALLY FATAL   YES

PREVENTABLE   SOMEWHAT

- Give your dog a full-body tick check every time your dog has been in the woods or high grass

> *For information on* **how to remove a tick** *see* **TICKS** *on page 46.*

- Spray lawn with vet-approved tick killer

- Keep lawn mowed

- Use a flea- and tick-preventative treatment (collar, dip, bath)

TREATABLE   YES

- With timely treatment, most dogs make a full recovery with no permanent damage to the nervous system

- Your vet will most likely prescribe tetracycline

SIGNS OF ROCKY MOUNTAIN SPOTTED FEVER

- Apathy

- Dizziness

- Fever

- Loss of appetite

- Muscle/joint pain

- Seizure

- Swelling in the face and legs

- Swollen lymph nodes

ticks

HOW TO REMOVE A TICK

- Separate your dog's fur so you can clearly see and reach the tick

- With a pair of tweezers, grasp the tick as close to its head (where it is attached to the body) as possible

- Pull firmly until the tick's entire body is removed from your dog's skin

- Flush the tick down the toilet

- Using a cotton ball, wipe the area with an antiseptic

- Wash your hands with soap and hot water

Note: Do **not** squeeze so hard on the tweezers that you decapitate the tick.
You do not want its head to remain burrowed in your dog.

WHAT **NOT** TO DO WHEN YOU FIND A TICK

- **DO NOT TRY TO BURN IT OFF**
  The current consensus is that you are more likely to burn yourself and your dog than actually succeed in removing the tick when you attempt to go the lit-match route.

- **DO NOT SMOTHER IT WITH VASELINE**
  Rumor had it that smothering a tick in Vaseline would force it to extricate its head from your dog's body to get air. However, all the Vaseline really succeeds in doing is killing the tick, which is not good while its head is still lodged in your dog.

west nile virus

POTENTIALLY FATAL **NOT TYPICALLY**
Dogs rarely catch West Nile Virus. When they do, they usually make a full recovery.

PREVENTABLE **NO**

TREATABLE **NO**
However, you can treat the symptoms with the sort of basic flu-therapy remedies you would use on a person: fluids, pain medication and rest

> - *According to the Center for Disease Control, West Nile Virus cannot be transmitted from dog to human, even if an infected dog bites the person.*

Notes . . . .

seasonal care for dogs of all ages

COLD-WEATHER TO DO LIST

- Buy your dog a coat
- Buy your dog booties
- Consider increasing the amount of food you give your dog. He actually burns more calories in cold weather keeping himself warm

COLD-WEATHER HAZARDS

> See the **CRITICAL CONDITIONS** section or **A-TO-Z DOG CARE REFERENCE** for treatment information.

- Frostbite
- Hypothermia
- Toxins
  - De-icing Salt
  - Antifreeze
  - Holiday foods
- Regional hazards . . . .
- Other . . . .

. . . .

If there is any chance your pup has come into contact with de-icing salt, be sure to wipe down his paws and stomach with a wet cloth as soon as you bring him inside. This will prevent him from ingesting toxins.

Pay attention to any leaks under your car. The same deadly toxin found in antifreeze is also in radiator coolant. If your car is leaking, be sure to get it checked as soon as possible and make sure your dog (and cat) does not have access to the spillage.

WARM-WEATHER TO DO LIST

- Start flea treatment
- Buy sunscreen for your dog

WARM-WEATHER HAZARDS

> See the **CRITICAL CONDITIONS** section or **A-TO-Z DOG CARE REFERENCE** for treatment information.

- Fleas and Ticks
- Heartworm
- Heat stroke
- Lyme Disease
- Sunburn
- Regional hazards . . . .
- Other . . . .

. . . .

Notes . . . .

. . . .

. . . .

. . . .

. . . .

. . . .

. . . .

puppy care

Few things in life are as joyful as getting a puppy. But with a puppy comes an enormous amount of responsibility and serious time commitment.

YOU WILL BE RESPONSIBLE FOR

- Vaccinations
- Housebreaking
- Training
- Licensing
- Spaying/neutering
- Puppy proofing your home

WORST TIMES TO GET A PUPPY

1. When you start a new job
2. When you know you'll be traveling a lot
3. When you are planning to move
4. When you or your spouse is pregnant
5. During the holidays

tips for puppy-proofing your house

- Tuck all cords away or encase them with cord covers to prevent your puppy from gnawing on electrical cords
- Place all plants out of reach
- Keep all cleaners and toxic chemicals out of reach
- Close doors or buy gates to block off rooms that are off-limits to your dog
- Keep valuable items, particularly clothes and shoes that carry your scent, out of reach
- Spray bitter apple on furniture to help prevent chewing
- Make sure windows are escape-proof
- Keep counters and tables free of food and anything else your puppy might be inclined to pull to the floor
- Do not put food, specifically chicken and turkey bones, in the trash if there is any way your puppy can get into it
- Keep bathroom doors closed to prevent your puppy from
    - Eating toilet paper
    - Digging through the waste basket
    - Drinking from the toilet
    - Getting into makeup, toiletries, soap and perfumes

puppy shopping list

ESSENTIALS FOR YOUR NEW DOG

- **COLLAR**

- **LEASH**

- **NAMETAG**

- **BOWLS** You'll need two, one for food and one for water. Stainless steel is easy to clean, indestructible and comes in many varieties. You can get a "no-tip" style, or elevated ones for taller breeds

- **DOG TREATS** For training purposes

- **PUPPY FOOD** Check with your veterinarian for a good brand to start your puppy on

- **GROOMING BRUSH** It is important to get your puppy used to being brushed and handled

- **PUPPY SHAMPOO** Puppies are notorious for geting into things, so have some gentle puppy shampoo on hand

- **NAIL CLIPPERS** If you get your puppy used to having his nails clipped when he is little, you won't have an issue when he is older. (For more information on **NAIL CLIP-PING** see **GROOMING TERMS**, page 71)

- **TOYS** Puppies need toys to chew on. Kong toys are great. Rawhide is not safe for dogs until they are at least a year old

- **CRATE** See **CRATE TRAINING**, page 53

- **BEDDING** Make sure it is machine washable and size appropriate

- **TOOTHBRUSH AND TOOTHPASTE** It is important to get your dog used to having you brush his teeth

- **CARPET STAIN REMOVER** For the inevitable potty training accidents

- **BITTER APPLE** Spray this on anything you don't want your dog to chew on, including furniture, electric cords, bandages, etc.

- **HOUSEBREAKING PADS**

- **POOP BAGS**

- . . . .

- . . . .

- . . . .

Notes . . . .

puppy vaccinations

As important as it is to begin socializing your puppy, you should keep your puppy away from unfamiliar dogs until he has had his final round of vaccination shots. Definitely do not visit dog parks until he is fully vaccinated.

DHLPP

This five-in-one shot series should be given every four weeks starting at eight weeks and ending at either 16 or 20 weeks. (Your veterinarian can give you a detailed vaccination schedule.)

DHLPP immunizes dogs against
- Distemper
- Hepatitis
- Leptospirosis
- Parainfluenza virus
- Parvovirus

DHLPP BOOSTER SHOTS

It used to be universally recommended that dogs be given a booster shot every year. However, there is some concern that over-vaccinating dogs can lead to serious health problems, including cancer. The general consensus now is that you should give your dog a booster shot at one year, then subsequently every three years until he is at least 10 years old. By that age, dogs that have received regular booster vaccinations will have developed a lifetime of immunity to the viruses. Be sure to speak to your vet before altering or stopping your dog's booster vaccination program.

Pet-care facilities take a very conservative approach to vaccinations. Generally, you are required to show proof of a booster vaccination within the last year before your dog can be admitted to a day-care or boarding facility.

RABIES

You are legally required to have your dog vaccinated against rabies. However, laws vary by state and city. Typically, the first vaccination expires after one year, with subsequent booster vaccinations required at three-year intervals.

Always keep your dog's rabies vaccination current! If an unvaccinated domestic animal is bitten by a wild animal, authorities recommend immediate euthanization. Dogs that have been vaccinated are usually quarantined for 10 days, while unvaccinated dogs are quarantined for up to six months if owners refuse to euthanize them.

KENNEL COUGH (CANINE BORDETELLA)

This vaccination is recommended at 12 to 16 weeks. However, it is optional and many people forgo it unless it is required by a day-care or boarding facility.

Kennel cough is highly contagious. As awful as a dog with kennel cough sounds, this condition is not life threatening. However, it can lead to serious secondary infections, including pneumonia.

For more information on **KENNEL COUGH**, see page 74.

housebreaking your dog

One of the not-so-fun parts of having a puppy is the inevitable puppy puddles you find during the housebreaking process. It is understandable to want to correct your puppy when you find a puddle. However, unless you catch your dog in the act, he will not have any idea what you are upset about. Punishing your dog or sticking his nose in the puddle won't do anything except confuse your dog and make him afraid of you. Wait until you catch him in the act, then firmly say "no," and quickly take him outside. Praise him as soon as he urinates outside.

TIPS FOR POTTY TRAINING YOUR PUPPY

- **Establish a schedule**

> **GETTING STARTED**
> *If your puppy does not eliminate the first time you take him outside, take him out every 30 minutes until he does. During the 30-minute interval(s), keep him either contained or on a leash, so you will be able to rush him outside if necessary. Once he has done his business, he should be okay for at least two hours. For puppies under six months, they can last one hour for each month of their lives. For example, a three-month-old puppy should be taken out every three hours.*

- Do not give your puppy water two hours before his bedtime

- Be patient. Dogs want to please you, and if you establish a routine, praise them for eliminating outdoors and are consistent—sooner or later, they will get it

> *Puppies need to go out every two to three hours, so be sure to hire a dog walker to walk your dog if you are unable to return home to let him out in a timely manner.*

- Good times to take your dog out for a potty break are
  - First thing in the morning
  - Anytime you let him out of his crate (if you are crate training)
  - After meals
  - After play time
  - After he wakes up from a nap
  - Whenever you return home
  - Before bedtime

- Praise your dog each time he eliminates outside

- Thoroughly clean spots where your dog has had accidents—dogs like to eliminate where they smell urine or feces

- Crate train your dog

Notes . . . .

crate training

New pet owners are often put off by the idea of "locking their puppy in a cage." However, used appropriately, a crate is not only humane, but it also promotes a more positive relationship between you and your dog. Many dogs enter their crates voluntarily because it represents a comfortable space and a crate-trained puppy doesn't have the opportunity to learn negative adult behaviors. (This may spare you the frustration of coming home to find a half-eaten chair or a new pair of shoes chewed to pieces.)

ADVANTAGES OF CRATE TRAINING

- Dogs are not given the opportunity to learn destructive behaviors

- Dogs do not like to soil where they sleep, so it makes the housebreaking process much easier

- It gives dogs a safe, quiet space when you have company or repairmen in the house

- Crate-trained dogs have a much easier time traveling

WHAT **NOT** TO DO WHILE CRATE TRAINING

- Do not put housebreaking pads in the crate. This will encourage your dog to eliminate in his crate

- Do not put your dog in the crate to punish him

- Do not let your puppy out of the crate while he is whining. Doing so will teach him to whine. Wait until he is quiet, then let him out of the crate

- During the day, do not leave your dog in his crate for more than four hours at a time. Puppies should be taken out every two to three hours until they reach five months. By this age they can usually wait four hours

CRATE SIZING

The crate should be long enough for your dog to stretch out, wide enough for your dog to completely turn around, and tall enough for him stand up without his head touching the top. Unless you plan to buy a new crate once your puppy is full grown, go ahead and buy the crate that will fit his anticipated size. When in doubt—go bigger rather than smaller. But be aware , if you go too big, a puppy may turn it into a two-bedroom condo with a bathroom in the back.

CRATE TRAINING TIPS

- Place something that contains your scent

KINDS OF CRATES		
TYPE	**PRO**	**CON**
COLLAPSIBLE WIRE MESH	easily transportable great air flow	hard to clean
WOODEN	attractive	hard to clean heavy
METAL	collapsible	heavy
PLASTIC	easy to clean lightweight	awkward to lift

(any article of dirty clothing will do) in the crate to help your dog relax

- Set aside a favorite chew toy and give it to your puppy only when he is in his crate

- Keep the crate in a room where people congregate, like the kitchen or family room (Dogs are pack animals and do not like to be isolated)

- Introduce your puppy to the crate early in the day, after a tiring play session. Start out with short five-to-ten minute sessions in the crate, gradually increasing the amount of time over the course of the day

- Put a few pieces of food or a treat in the crate so your dog will enter voluntarily

- Make sure your dog gets plenty of exercise before and after he is in his crate

top reasons to spay/neuter

- Spaying and neutering helps reduce the animal-population problem

- Spayed/neutered animals live up to three years longer than their unaltered counterparts

- By spaying or neutering your animal, you get a significant discount on the cost of licensing your dog

- Spaying your female dog before her first estrus cycle greatly reduces her chances of getting breast cancer and eliminates the possibility of uterine and ovarian cancers

- Neutered males are less aggressive than non-neutered males

- Neutered males are less likely to "mark their territory" by spraying

- Neutered males are less likely to roam/run away than unaltered males

- Neutered males are less likely to bite—the majority of dog bites come from unaltered males

> *Each year eight-million animals are euthanized because they do not have homes. By spaying/neutering your dog, you are doing your part to help curb the pet overpopulation crisis.*

Notes

adult dog care

Adult dogs are relatively low maintenance. Please consider the following measures to help your dog maintain optimum health.

- **ROUTINE CHECKUPS** By taking your dog in for annual exams, you have a better chance of catching disease and problems in the early stages

- **DIET** By maintaining your dog's weight at a healthy level, you prevent a whole host of problems later on

- **EXERCISE** Whether you share a morning run, enjoy tossing him the Frisbee or prefer to watch him play with other dogs in the park, your dog needs regular exercise to stay healthy and happy

- **FLEA AND TICK PREVENTION** Administer monthly flea treatment year round in warmer climates and from early spring through late fall in cooler climates

- **NUTRITION** When it comes to dog food, you get what you pay for. The cheaper dog-food brands provide dogs with about as much nutritional value as children receive from sugar-coated cereals

- **ORAL HYGIENE** Schedule regular teeth cleaning appointments for your dog. Most vets will only do teeth cleaning under anesthesia. However, many pet-supply stores now offer anesthesia-free teeth cleaning through outside providers. (For more information, see **DENTAL HYGIENE** in the **A-TO-Z DOG CARE REFERENCE**, page 66)

- **VACCINATIONS** Get your dog vaccinated every one to three years, depending on what you and your vet agree upon

- **VET CARE** If you notice anything unusual, get it checked out with your vet right away. Many vets will answer questions over the phone for regular clients

> *To reduce the number of times your dog is anesthetized, you might consider getting his teeth cleaned any time he requires anesthesia for another procedure. You may also want to consider anesthesia-free teeth cleaning.*

HOW TO FIND A HEALTHY DOG FOOD FOR YOUR DOG

- Avoid dog foods that are available in supermarkets—look for a brand that is sold in pet-supply stores

- Ask the store owners or managers what their top picks are as well as why they prefer one over another

- Read the label

- Natural preservatives (Vitamin E) are better than chemical preservatives

- Ingredients are listed in order, with primary ingredients listed first—avoid foods where vegetables, especially corn, are listed as the first ingredient

Note: When you change your dog's food, do it gradually, slowly replacing the old brand with the new food.

> *If you decide to feed your dog a raw-food diet, ask your vet to recommend an appropriate vitamin and mineral supplement. For more information, see **BONES AND RAW FOOD DIET (BARF)** in the **A-TO-Z DOG CARE REFERENCE**, page 59.*

senior dog care

Acknowledging the signs that your dog is growing old is about as fun as finding your first gray hair. However, the earlier you address the fact that your pup is aging, the more you can do to sustain his quality of life and prevent, or at least delay, disease.

> **AT WHAT AGE DOES YOUR DOG QUALIFY AS SENIOR?**
>
> *Dogs enter their senior years at different ages, depending on their size and breed. Generally speaking, a small dog is considered to be senior at 12 years, while a larger dog may be considered senior as early as six years. Your vet can tell you when it is appropriate to start screening your dog for geriatric health issues.*

MEASURES YOU CAN TAKE TO STAY ON TOP OF YOUR PET'S HEALTH

- **ACUPUNCTURE AND CHIROPRACTICS** Consider scheduling treatments for your dog to help alleviate arthritis

- **DENTAL HYGIENE** Brush your dog's teeth and schedule regular teeth-cleaning appointments—tooth decay and gum disease can lead to a slew of other health problems

- **DIET** Watch your dog's weight! As dogs age, their metabolism slows, which means they burn fewer calories and require less food

- **DOG BED** Invest in a dog bed that offers your dog plenty of support. Place the bed in a dry, draft-free spot, preferably off the floor

- **EXERCISE** Modify—but don't cut out—your dog's exercise regimen

- **GROOMING** Brush and groom your dog regularly to help him maintain a healthy coat

- **KNOW YOUR DOG** Be aware of, and on the lookout for, illnesses and issues that are typical of your dog's breed

- **MASSAGE** Give your dog regular massage treatments to improve circulation and ease tension, aches and pains. If you do not want to pay for regular massage treatments, take a class or schedule a canine massage therapist for a one-time visit to teach you how to work on your dog yourself

- **NUTRITION** Feed your dog high-quality food to help him maintain optimal health

- **RAMPS, STEPS AND SKID-PROOF FLOORING** Consider purchasing a ramp to help your dog get in and out of the car, steps to help your dog get on and off furniture, and skid-proof carpeting to prevent your dog from slipping on slippery surfaces and stairs

- **ROUTINE CHECKUPS** Increase the frequency of your pup's routine exam to every six to eight months

- **SUPPLEMENTS** Consider giving your dog
  - Glucosamine sulfate and chondritin (for arthritis)
  - Vitamin and mineral supplements (for overall health)
  - Omega fatty acid (for coat)
  - Glycerin (for eyes)

  Consult your vet for proper dosage information

- **VACCINATIONS** Reduce the frequency of your dog's vaccinations to every three years. With the approval of your vet, you may consider stopping vaccinations altogether when your dog turns 10 years old

canine cognitive dysfunction syndrome (CDS)

Dogs lose some cognitive ability as they age, and at one time or another, most will exhibit one or two of the symptoms of CDS. However, these behaviors are not a normal part of the aging process. If your dog exhibits more than a couple of these symptoms, and your vet has ruled out other causes, you should get your dog checked for CDS.

SIGNS OF CDS

- **CONFUSION** Getting turned around or lost in the house or backyard, or not recognizing an owner or caretaker

- **CHANGE IN BEHAVIOR PATTERNS** Being apathetic about receiving affection from an owner or caretaker, or not bothering to come when called by owner

- **CHANGE IN SLEEP PATTERNS** Sleeping more during the day and less at night

- **HOUSE-TRAINING REGRESSION** Having accidents, forgetting to ask to go outside

TREATMENT

While there is no cure for CDS, the symptoms are treatable with a medication called Anipril, which increases the amount of dopamine going to the brain while decreasing the production of free radicals. Like most medications, Anipril is not without its side effects, so carefully weigh the pros and cons with your veterinarian before starting your dog on this medication.

when to see your vet

Unfortunately, despite preventative measures, older dogs are more prone to illness and disease. If your dog has any of the following symptoms, schedule an appointment with your vet as soon as possible.

- Abnormal swelling or lumps
- Bleeding or discharge from any body opening
- Difficulty defecating
- Difficulty eating or swallowing
- Difficulty or reluctance to do routine activities
- Difficulty urinating
- Excessive panting
- Increased thirst/water intake
- Increased urination
- Offensive body odor
- Significant loss of appetite
- Sores that don't heal
- Sudden change in activity level
- Unexplained diarrhea or vomiting that lasts longer than a day
- Unexplained exhaustion or apathy
- Unexplained stiffness or lameness
- Unexplained weight loss

For information on specific conditions, diseases and illnesses, see **CRITICAL CONDITIONS** and the **A-TO-Z DOG CARE REFERENCE**.

IF YOUR DOG REQUIRES MEDICAL ATTENTION, CONTACT YOUR VET OR ANIMAL EMERGENCY FACILITY IMMEDIATELY.

when dogs go to heaven

The disparity between our dog's lifespan and our own is one of the great injustices in this world. Losing a pet is a very sad, sometimes devastating, experience. Many people do not realize how much they will be affected until it happens. If you are too overcome with grief to deal with the logistics, many veterinarians' offices will handle all of the arrangements for you, including picking up your pet and having him cremated or buried. It may seem like a morbid thing to do, but it might be a good idea to ask your vet in advance what her policies are. Then, when the need arises, you will know to what degree you can count on your vet to handle the situation.

EUTHANASIA

The decision to put an animal to sleep is one of the most difficult a person must make. The fact that it may be the most humane thing to do does not make it any easier. You may want to consult with your vet, and perhaps someone else that you trust, and ask them to help you determine if it is the right time and the right thing to do for your dog.

If you decide euthanasia is the best thing to do, many people prefer to have a vet come to their house to put their dog to sleep. This way, their dog can spend his final moments in the comfort of his home. In many instances, the vet will give the animal a sedative prior to the euthanasia injection. Ask your vet if this is standard procedure. If it is not, ask the vet to prescribe a sedative for your dog that you can give him prior to the vet's arrival. If your vet will not perform in-home euthanasia, ask her for a recommendation of someone who provides this service.

FINAL ARRANGEMENTS

A reputable pet funeral home or crematorium should treat you and your dog with compassion and respect as well as provide you with options that fit your financial situation.

Notes . . . .

. . . .

. . . .

. . . .

. . . .

. . . .

. . . .

pet loss

BOOKS

Coping with Sorrow on the Loss of Your Pet 2nd Edition by Moira Anderson. Loveland, CO, Alpine Publications 1996

The Loss of a Pet by Wallace Sife, Ph.D. rev. ed. NY Howell Book House 1998

Pet Loss: A Thoughtful Guide for Adults and Children by Herbert Nieberg, Ph.D. NY, Harper & Row 1996

HOTLINES

THE ANIMAL MEDICAL CENTER
(212) 838-8100
New York, NY

COLORADO STATE UNIVERSITY
(303) 221-4535
College of Veterinary Medicine
Fort Collins, CO

UNIVERSITY OF CALIFORNIA AT DAVIS
(530) 752-4200
School of Veterinary Medicine
Davis, CA

UNIVERSITY OF MINNESOTA
(612) 624-4747
College of Veterinary Medicine
St. Paul, MO

THE UNIVERSITY OF PENNSYLVANIA
(215) 898-4529
School of Veterinary Medicine
Philadelphia, PA

WASHINGTON STATE UNIVERSITY
(509) 335-1297
College of Veterinary Medicine
Pullman, WA

INTERNET SUPPORT

THE ASSOCIATION FOR PET LOSS AND BEREAVEMENT
(718) 382-0960
www.aplb.org

The Association for Pet Loss and Bereavement (APLB) was founded in 1987 by psychologist Wallace Sife—author of The Loss of a Pet—*after he lost his own dog and realized there was nowhere to turn to process his grief. Today APLB is a nationwide database with everything from cemeteries and support groups to lawyers specializing in pet-related wrongful-action cases.*

Notes . . . .

. . . .

. . . .

. . . .

. . . .

acupuncture

The ancient healing art of acupuncture dates back over 3000 years. Based upon the idea that infirmity blocks "chi," or life force, acupuncture involves the placement of fine needles in specific points along your dog's body. The goal is to balance your dog's energy system by dispersing blockages, alleviating pain and restoring optimum health. Animals undergoing acupuncture often sink into a restful, sleepy state, most likely because of increased endorphine levels that the treatment is said to produce.

HEALTH ISSUES THAT MAY BE TREATED WITH ACUPUNCTURE INCLUDE

- Allergies
- Arthritis
- Gastrointestinal problems
- Hip dysplasia
- Kidney problems
- Spinal disorders

Acupuncture is a gradual process—your pet may need several treatments to show signs of improvement. Though considered alternative therapy, acupuncture is becoming increasingly popular among vets, many of whom claim to observe increased alertness, playfulness and better overall health in treated patients.

Even if your pet is not exhibiting symptoms of illness, his energy points can be examined and checked for blockages or misalignment. Areas that might become problematic in the future can be targeted and treated, minimizing or possibly even preventing future pain and infirmity.

For more information on acupuncture for your dog, go to
- acupuncture.com/animals
- animalhealthpractice.com/acupuncture

In no way is this book meant to replace emergency and/or routine veterinary care. The content of this book is designed for informational purposes only.

IF YOUR DOG REQUIRES MEDICAL ATTENTION, CONTACT YOUR VET OR ANIMAL EMERGENCY FACILITY IMMEDIATELY.

Notes . . . .

allergies

FOOD ALLERGIES

The most common foods that produce allergic reactions in dogs are

- Beef
- Chicken
- Corn
- Eggs
- Fish
- Milk
- Pork
- Soy
- Whey

SIGNS OF AN ALLERGIC REACTION TO FOOD CAN INCLUDE

- Diarrhea
- Gas
- Seizures
- Skin outbreaks
- Vomiting

FOOD ELIMINATION DIET

Determining which ingredient is causing the allergic reaction requires putting your dog on a food-elimination diet. For this diet to be successful, you need to be hyper-vigilant about preventing your dog from eating any food that is not on the diet. This diet should only be implemented under the supervision of a veterinarian.

For an eight-to-10-week period, put your dog on a protein/carbohydrate diet along with a hypo-allergenic nutritional supplement. If you want to make the food yourself, combine any protein your dog has never had before (such as venison) with rice. However, several dog-food brands now offer hypoallergenic foods.

If all of your dog's symptoms disappear, you can assume your dog has an allergy to an ingredient in his previous diet. At this point, you have two choices: you can either avoid all of the ingredients in that food, or do an eight-week test on each ingredient until you find the allergen.

TIPS TO HELP PREVENT ALLERGIC REACTIONS

- Change your dog's diet frequently but gradually by mixing old food with new food to challenge his immune system

- Always feed your dog in a clean, stainless-steel bowl

- Feed your dog a diet that is free of artificial flavors, dyes and preservatives

Notes . . . .

. . . .

. . . .

. . . .

arthritis

Arthritis is the term used to describe any number of degenerative joint diseases in which symptoms include pain, swelling and stiffness. In dogs, arthritis usually takes the form of hip dysplasia, elbow dysplasia, joint degeneration or dislocation of the knee.

SIGNS OF ARTHRITIS

- Apathy

- Decreased energy

- Difficulty or hesitation when jumping on furniture

- Difficulty or hesitation when climbing stairs

- Slowed movement

- Weight gain

TREATMENT

Prescription anti-inflammatory medications are available but usually requires a blood test to check your dog's liver and kidney functions. Talk to your vet about potential side effects before starting this or any medications.

Aspirin is sometimes recommended. However, you should not give your dog aspirin without explicit approval and dosage instructions from your vet.

> **UNDER NO CIRCUMSTANCES SHOULD YOU EVER GIVE YOUR DOG IBUPROFEN (ADVIL, MOTRIN) NAPROXIN (ALEVE), OR ACETAMINOPHEN (TYLENOL). THESE MEDICATIONS ARE VERY TOXIC TO YOUR DOG.**

> See **SENIOR DOG CARE**, page 55, for more information on measures you can take that will help alleviate your dog's arthritis.

Notes . . . .

. . . .

. . . .

. . . .

. . . .

. . . .

bee stings

Usually, dogs are protected from bees and wasps by their coats. However, the nose, mouth, paws and sometimes the abdomen are vulnerable.

SIGNS YOUR DOG HAS BEEN STUNG INCLUDE
- Biting at paws
- Extreme agitation
- Rubbing muzzle with paws
- Shaking head
- Swelling (will start within minutes and worsen over the next 30 to 60 minutes)

WHAT TO DO IF YOUR DOG GETS STUNG
- Examine your dog
- If you find the stinger, remove it ASAP with a pair of sterilized tweezers
- Do not panic if you cannot find the stinger —dogs can dislodge it on their own
- Call your vet so she can advise you as to whether you need to come in or if you can treat your dog at home

CONVENTIONAL TREATMENT
Note: Ask your vet for dosage information
- Children's Benadril (antihistamine)
- Cortisone cream (topical, reduces itching)

ALTERNATIVE TREATMENT
Note: Speak to your alternative vet for dosage information
- Calendula (topical, reduces itching)
- Homeopathic Apis (reduces swelling)
- Rescue Remedy (treats shock)

> IF YOUR DOG APPEARS TO HAVE BEEN STUNG IN THE MOUTH, CALL YOUR VET OR ANIMAL EMERGENCY FACILITY ASAP. A STING IN THE MOUTH CAN CAUSE AN OBSTRUCTION OF THE AIRWAY, AND YOUR DOG MAY REQUIRE AN ANTIHISTA-MINE OR STEROID SHOT.

bloat

See **CRITICAL CONDITIONS**, page 38.

bones and raw food (BARF) diet

There is a lot of controversy surrounding raw-food diets. Advocates of BARF claim that raw meat—the type of food dogs, as carnivores, would seek out if they lived in the wild—adds years to dogs' lives. Additionally, they believe that changing from a processed- to a raw-food diet can cure a multitude of ailments such as allergies, lethargy and anxiety.

Opponents of BARF argue that there is no scientific evidence to substantiate the claims made by the pro-BARF camp and that this diet exposes dogs to serious health risks.

IF YOU DECIDE TO SWITCH YOUR DOG OVER TO A RAW-FOOD DIET
- Do so under the supervision of a licensed veterinarian
- Consider adding vitamin and mineral supplements to your dog's diet
- Plan to make a serious commitment of both time and money

Notes . . . .

cancer

Like people, dogs can develop several types of cancer, including bone, blood vessel, breast, bladder, urethra and anal gland.

Treatments for animals with cancer are similar to those for people: chemotherapy and radiation therapy. Herbal supplements are also used to combat various cancers.

PREVENTION

- Spay your female dog before she goes through her first heat
- Make sure your dog gets plenty of exercise
- Keep your pet's diet low in sugar (both simple and complex) and high in protein and fatty acids

TREATMENTS

- Chemotherapy
- Radiation therapy
- Holistic treatments
  - Supplements
  - Coenzyme Q10
  - Artemisinin
  - Aloe Vera injections

WHEN TO SEE THE VET

If your dog exhibits any of the following symptoms, schedule an appointment with your vet ASAP

- Abnormal swelling
- Bleeding or discharge from any body opening
- Difficulty breathing, urinating or defecating
- Difficulty eating or swallowing
- Loss of appetite
- Offensive body odor
- Sores that won't heal
- Unexplained exhaustion
- Unexplained stiffness or lameness
- Unexplained weight loss

Alternative therapies like acupuncture and chiropractics are much more effective at preventing rather than treating cancer.

Notes . . . .

. . . .

. . . .

. . . .

. . . .

. . . .

car sickness

For many dogs, vomiting is not a result of motion sickness so much as a manifestation of anxiety.

SIGNS THAT YOUR DOG MAY VOMIT

- Excessive drooling
- Excessive yawning

WHAT TO DO IF YOUR DOG GETS CARSICK

- Crack a window to provide your dog with fresh air
- If possible, have your dog lie down on the floor—sometimes looking out the window can cause car sickness
- If you can safely get out of the car, take your dog for a short walk

HOW TO PREVENT CAR SICKNESS

- Make sure to have your pet travel on an empty stomach
- Help your dog adjust to the car by taking him on frequent short trips
- If your dog is prone to car sickness and you are going on a long drive, consider giving him a motion-sickness medication such as Dramamine (consult your vet about proper dosages)

> **IF YOUR DOG REQUIRES MEDICAL ATTEN-TION, CONTACT YOUR VET OR ANIMAL EMERGENCY FACILITY IMMEDIATELY.**

cataracts

Cataracts, defined as cloudiness of the eye lense, appears as a white coating covering the pupil. The most common form of cataracts is senile cataracts, which is a natural result of aging. This type, which usually affects both eyes at once, is pronounced. When younger dogs develop cataracts, it is usually due to a nutritional deficiency, infection or trauma to the eye.

PREVENTION

A good way to slow the development and progression of cataracts is to supplement your pet's diet with vitamins E and C.

TREATMENT

Cataracts can be corrected surgically by a veterinarian.

DOGS MOST LIKELY TO GET CATARACTS

- Chesapeake Bay retrievers
- Cocker spaniels
- German shepherds
- Huskies
- Old English sheepdogs
- Poodles
- Retrievers
- Schnauzers
- Springer spaniels
- Westies

If you notice that your pet has developed cataracts, don't panic—cataracts often look worse than they actually are. Cataracts in dogs aren't quite as problematic as they are for people. Since dogs rely heavily on their sense of smell, they function relatively well with less than perfect vision.

chiropractics

Chiropractic treatment is the physical manipulation of the spinal column and musculoskeletal system in order to produce optimal balance in the body. While a series of chiropractic treatments is frequently recommended, a chiropractic adjustment often provides a dog with instant pain relief and increased mobility.

SKELETAL SYSTEM AND JOINTS

When all the vertebrae are in alignment, the dog is capable of pain-free movement and flexibility. When one or more of the joints fall out of alignment, the joints can become stiff or sore, decreasing the dog's mobility.

MUSCULAR SYSTEM

When joints are out of alignment they put undue pressure on the muscles, causing spasms, knots and, over time, degeneration. Conversely, weak muscles that do not properly support the skeletal system can cause joints to fall out of alignment.

NERVOUS SYSTEM

Nerves direct communication between the brain and all other areas of the body. When one or more joints fall out of alignment, the nerves can become blocked and/or pinched.

CHIROPRACTIC TREATMENT

Chiropractic treatment can be extremely beneficial for dogs suffering from discomfort in the skeletal, muscular or nervous system. All three systems are so interconnected that adjusting one (the skeletal system) almost always positively affects the other two (the muscular and nervous systems).

cushing's disease

Cushing's disease is the result of adrenal gland over-production, usually brought on by a pituitary tumor (85% of cases), an adrenal tumor or by chronic steroid use.

SIGNS OF CUSHING'S DISEASE INCLUDE

- Bulging, sagging abdomen
- Hair loss
- High blood pressure
- Increased appetite
- Increased drinking
- Increased urination
- Muscle weakness
- Panting
- Skin lumps
- Thin skin

BREEDS MOST AT RISK

- Dachshunds
- German shepherds
- Golden retrievers
- Standard poodles
- Terriers

TREATMENT

Treatment varies depending on the cause of the disease. In some instances, Cushing's disease can be treated with medication, in other cases, the adrenal glands are removed. Your vet is the best person to advise you about treatment options.

Notes . . . .

. . . .

. . . .

. . . .

dental hygiene

Dogs are just as susceptible as people are to gingivitis and tooth decay. And just like people, periodontal disease in dogs can lead to serious health conditions, including heart disease.

HOW TO PREVENT TOOTH DECAY AND PERI-ODONTAL DISEASE IN YOUR DOG

- Feed your dog dry—as opposed to wet—food

- Give your dog bones and rawhide to chew on (under supervision)

- Brush your dog's teeth

- Give your dog mouthwash (you can get it from your vet)

- Schedule regular anesthesia-free teeth cleaning appointments

- If your dog has to go under anesthesia for another procedure, consider scheduling ultrasonic teeth cleaning at the same time

- Have your vet remove decaying teeth

REASONS YOUR DOG MAY HAVE BAD BREATH

- Tartar and plaque (yellow/green buildup on the surface of the teeth)

- Mouth infection

- Losing baby teeth (puppies)

- Kidney and liver disease

WHEN TO PUT AWAY THE BREATH MINTS AND SEE THE VET

- When your dog's breath smells fruity or sweet. This is an indicator of diabetes

- When your dog's breath is unusually foul. This is an indicator of internal health problems or advanced tooth decay

Notes . . . .

. . . .

. . . .

. . . .

. . . .

. . . .

. . . .

. . . .

ear infections

Ear infections can be caused by several things

- Allergies
- Bacteria/yeast
- Foreign objects in the ear (debris, dirt, mites, ticks)
- Fungus
- Hypothyroidism (low thyroid function)
- Tumor
- Water trapped in the ear

PREVENTION

- Make sure to check your dog for ticks when he returns from the woods or tall grass
- Clean the inner ear flap and the outer part of the ear canal with rubbing alcohol or canine ear cleansing solution. Use a cotton ball or gauze pad
- Check ears at least once a week
- If your dog gets chronic ear infections, speak to your vet about possible underlying causes

TREATMENT

Your dog needs to be seen by a vet so that he can be properly diagnosed and given the appropriate medicine for his specific infection. Once he has been diagnosed, treatment is very simple

- Ear drops or ointment
- Removal of foreign object in the ear

SIGNS OF AN EAR INFECTION

- Black or yellowish discharge
- Ear scratching
- Ear wax
- Head shaking
- Red and/or inflamed ears
- Smelly ears

Dogs with long floppy ears that block air from getting into the ear are more prone to ear infections. Following is a list of breeds that are predisposed to ear infections

- Basset hounds
- Cocker spaniels
- Irish setters
- Labradors
- Poodles

> **UNDER NO CIRCUMSTANCES SHOULD YOU EVER TRY TO REMOVE AN OBJECT THAT IS LODGED IN YOUR DOG'S EAR. TAKE YOUR DOG TO YOUR VET OR ANIMAL EMERGENCY FACILITY ASAP.**

> **IF YOUR DOG REQUIRES MEDICAL ATTENTION, CONTACT YOUR VET OR ANIMAL EMERGENCY FACILITY IMMEDIATELY.**

Notes . . . .

. . . .

. . . .

first-aid kit

You should keep a dog first-aid kit on hand for emergencies.

The following companies make comprehensive first-aid kits that you can purchase.

Healerpetproducts.com
- Home Pet Pak First-Aid Kit
- Travel Pet Pak First-aid Kit

Medipet.com
- Medi+Pet Deluxe First-Aid Kit
- Medi+Pet Standard First-Aid Kit
- Medi+Pet Travel First-Aid Kit

If you decide to make your own first-aid kit, you should consider stocking it with the following medications and first-aid supplies.

MEDICINE

Note: Always speak to your vet and confirm dosage information before giving human medication to your dog.

- Aspirin
- Benadryl (Children's)
- Hydrogen Peroxide (to induce vomiting)
- Immodium
- Mineral oil (laxative)
- Pedialyte (dehydration)
- Pepto Bismol

> **UNDER NO CIRCUMSTANCES SHOULD YOU EVER GIVE YOUR DOG IBUPROFEN (ADVIL, MOTRIN) NAPROXIN (ALEVE), OR ACETAMINOPHEN (TYLENOL). THESE MEDICATIONS ARE VERY TOXIC TO YOUR DOG.**

FIRST-AID SUPPLIES

- Ace bandage
- Antibacterial soap
- Antibiotic ointment (such as Betadine)
- Antiseptic wipes
- Band-aids
- Blanket (to preserve body heat)
- Blunt-edge scissors
- Bottled water
- Canine thermometer
- Disposable cold compress pack (for swelling)
- Disposable hot compress pack
- Cotton balls
- Cotton gauze pad
- Cotton gauze roll
- Cotton swabs
- Eye rinsing solution
- First-aid tape
- Gloves (for you to handle open wounds)
- Honey packet/sugar (dehydration, shock/ hypothermia)
- Hot water bottle
- Liquid bandages (good for paw abrasions)
- Matches
- Needle and thread
- Oral syringes
  Note: Insert the syringe between your dog's teeth, don't aim at his throat
- Rubbing alcohol
- Safety pins

- Tweezers
- Vaseline
- ....
- ....
- ....

- Ear infection ointment
- Extra dosages of any meds your dog is taking
- Eye infection ointment
- Hot spot remedies
- Hydrocortisone topical spray

Notes ....

fleas

The best way to prevent a flea infestation is to be consistent with your dog's flea-prevention medication. Frontline, Advantage and Revolution are the three top brands—each offers user-friendly topical treatments. You can also use a flea collar or spray (Frontline has a good one).

If your dog gets fleas, you can pretty much count on your house being infested too. Act fast!

Treatment of a flea infestation must be done on several levels. Depending on the severity of the situation, you can do any or all of the following

- Treat your dog. Medications include topical ointments (Frontline, Advantage or Revolution), flea dips and flea shampoos

- Vacuum all rugs, carpet and upholstery

- Wash all flea-exposed bedding, clothing and linens in soapy, hot water

- Set off a flea bomb or fogger (be sure to keep people and animals out of area for the designated time period!)

- Use a flea powder

- Keep your grass mowed and treat your yard with an insecticide

> WHEN FLEA BOMBING YOUR HOME, CLOSE OFF ANY ROOMS THAT HAVE NOT BEEN INFESTED AND REMOVE ALL PEOPLE AND ANIMALS FROM THE HOUSE.

FLEA BOMBING

Flea foggers are incredibly toxic. That is why they are so effective in killing fleas. Before you fog your house, take the following precautions

- **KITCHEN** Completely cover or remove all food, utensils, dishware, glasses, silverware, etc.

- **BATHROOM** Completely cover or remove all tissue, toilet paper, towels, wash clothes, toothbrushes, toiletries, makeup, brushes, etc.

- **BEDROOM** Remove all sheets and pillow cases and completely cover or remove all clothes

> IF YOUR DOG REQUIRES MEDICAL ATTENTION, CONTACT YOUR VET OR ANIMAL EMERGENCY FACILITY IMMEDIATELY.

Notes . . . .

. . . .

. . . .

. . . .

rostbite

See **CRITICAL CONDITIONS**, *page 39.*

rooming terms

SANITARY CLIP

Refers to clipping around the dog's genital and anal areas to ensure that the areas are kept clean

ANAL GLAND EXPRESSION

Refers to the removal of the fluid inside the dog's anal glands. Every dog has anal glands (about the size of grapes) that are located on either side of the anus. These glands fill up with a thick fluid that is usually expressed when the dog defecates. However, smaller breeds sometimes have trouble with this and need to have their anal glands expressed. Non-expressed anal glands can lead to anal-gland impaction and disease

TRIMMING PAW FUR

Refers to the clipping down of fur between toes and around the paws. This is to make sure the area stays clean and matt-free. Without care, paws can get matted and un-comfortable, and debris can stick to the feet and cause pain

EAR CLEANING

Refers to the trimming of the fur around and just inside the ear flaps to keep the area clean and bacteria free. Dirty ears can become infected

NAIL TRIMMING

Refers to nail clipping. Dogs that do not wear down their own nails through natural use need their nails clipped every four to six weeks. Long nails can get caught and rip or grow into the paw. Both of these scenarios are very painful and can lead to infection

Notes . . . .

. . . .

. . . .

. . . .

. . . .

. . . .

. . . .

. . . .

heartworm

See **CRITICAL CONDITIONS**, *page 40.*

heat stroke

See **CRITICAL CONDITIONS**, *page 41.*

homeopathy

Homeopathy is an alternative approach to medicine. In homeopathic treatment, medication is administered to exacerbate pre-existing symptoms of illness, which induces the body to heal itself. The objective in homeopathy is to completely cure the underlying illness, rather than manage the symptoms through medication.

Notes . . . .

. . . .

. . . .

. . . .

. . . .

. . . .

. . . .

. . . .

hookworms

Dogs get hookworm from walking on soil, grass or beaches that are infested with hookworm larvae. The hookworm burrows into the dog's skin. Once inside the dog, it journeys to the intestine, where it matures.

CAN IT BE PASSED FROM DOG TO PERSON?
Yes. The larvae can burrow into your skin and cause "ground itch," but hookworms do not mature in people.

PREVENTION
• Promptly pick up and dispose of dog waste

• Wash your hands after disposing of dog waste

• Promptly de-worm infected pet(s)

TREATMENT
It is necessary to administer injections or oral tablets twice over a month-long period since the medication only works on adult hookworms, not larvae.

SIGNS OF HOOKWORMS
• Anemia

• Bloody diarrhea

• Pale gums

• Skin irritation

• Thinning coat

• Weight loss

DOGS MOST LIKELY TO GET HOOKWORM
• Puppies

HOW DO DOGS GET HOOKWORMS?
• Through the skin (mostly the footpads) by touching contaminated feces or damp soil

• Through the mother's placenta (before birth)

• From their mother's milk

hypothermia

See **CRITICAL CONDITIONS**, *page 42.*

insurance, pet

Pet insurance serves as a safeguard against expensive medical bills resulting from unforeseeable conditions such as cancer, broken bones and emergency surgical procedures.

Generally, you are required to pay a $50 deductible for each visit to the vet or emergency room.

You can also purchase an add-on plan, which provides an allowance for routine care visits such as annual exams, vaccinations and teeth cleanings. If you want to purchase pet insurance, consider doing it while your dog is a puppy—before he has time to develop any "pre-existing conditions."

HOW PET INSURANCE IS LIKE PEOPLE INSURANCE

- Monthly payments ($15-$70)
- Pre-existing conditions are not covered
- There is a deductible ($50) for each visit

HOW PET INSURANCE IS **NOT** LIKE PEOPLE INSURANCE

- You can choose any licensed veterinarian you like (no network to navigate)
- Discounts for multiple pets (you receive about 10% off for each additional plan)
- You must pay your entire bill up-front and file a claim to get reimbursed

NATIONAL PET INSURANCE COMPANIES

- petinsurance.com
- petcareinsurance.com

> **IF YOUR DOG REQUIRES MEDICAL ATTENTION, CONTACT YOUR VET OR ANIMAL EMERGENCY FACILITY IMMEDIATELY.**

Notes . . . .

kennel cough

PREVENTION

- Immunization
- Don't share your dog's toys or bowls with unfamiliar dogs
- Make sure your dog's kennel is adequately ventilated

TREATMENT

- Antibiotics
- Cough suppressants

SIGNS OF KENNEL COUGH

- Conjunctivitis
- Dry, hacking cough
- Nasal discharge
- Retching and expulsion of white foamy discharge after coughing

DOGS MOST LIKELY TO GET KENNEL COUGH

- Dogs who travel frequently
- Show dogs
- Dogs who stay at kennels frequently

legal aid

The sad truth is that we live in an increasingly litigious world, and there are myriad reasons why you might need a pet attorney to represent you, including

- Estate planning for your pet(s)
- Disputes with landlords or neighbors
- Filing a malpractice suit
- Your dog being attacked by or attacking another dog
- Disputes with animal control

Check the **ANIMAL LEGAL DEFENSE FUND** website for a list of lawyers (sorted by state) who practice animal law exclusively (aldf.org).

For more information about animal legal aid, pick up *Dog Law*, 4th ed. by Mary Randolph (Nolo 2001).

lyme disease

See **CRITICAL CONDITIONS**, *page 43.*

Notes . . . .

. . . .

nail trimming

Unless your dog gets plenty of activity on hard surfaces, you will most likely need to clip his nails. If this is something you plan on doing yourself, start as early as possible. You have the best chance of desensitizing your dog to this process while he is still a puppy.

Some dogs handle having their nails trimmed better than others. If your dog has particularly sensitive nails, you will save yourself and your dog a lot of aggravation by having a groomer or vet tech trim his nails. They will be able to get the ordeal over with more quickly, and if nail clipping is a truly negative experience for your dog, you do not want him to associate it with you.

Unless they wear them down on their own, most dogs need their nails trimmed at least once a month.

HOW TO USE A DOG NAIL TRIMMER
- Spread your dog's toes
- Cut from underneath the nail, not from the top down
- Make sure there is plenty of light so you do not cut too much of the nail. (The pink part of the nail is alive in dogs with white nails. The darker part of the nail is alive in dogs with black nails)
- Make each cut a smooth squeeze with the nail trimmers
- You can file the edges down or let your dog wear them down

WHAT TO DO IF YOU CUT TOO SHORT AND THE NAIL STARTS BLEEDING
- Press a tissue to the bottom of the nail
- Apply a syptic powder (available at pet stores) to the bottom of the nail

pancreatitis

See **CRITICAL CONDITIONS**, *page 44.*

rattlesnakes

See **CRITICAL CONDITIONS**, *page 45.*

ringworm

Despite its name, ringworm actually has nothing to do with worms. It's a fungus that takes the shape of a puffy ring. Symptoms of ringworm are most apparent on the face, ear tips, tail and paws.

SIGNS OF RINGWORM
- Circular patches of hair loss
- Scaly, reddened skin
- The signature ring

RINGWORM IS HIGHLY CONTAGIOUS—DOGS CAN CATCH IT FROM
- Cats
- Contaminated grooming supplies
- Digging in soil where the fungus is present
- Other dogs
- People
- Rodents

TREATMENT
- Anti-fungal shampoo
- Griseofulvin tablets (prescription)
- Lime sulfur dips
- Topical anti-fungal medication

Note: In some instances, your vet may recommend shaving the hair around the ringworm to prevent further spreading and promote healing.

rocky mountain spotted fever

See **CRITICAL CONDITIONS**, page 45.

roundworms

Roundworms are parasitic worms that live off of partially digested food. Dogs swallow the eggs. The larvae hatch in the dog's stomach, then travel to the intestine, where the mature worms (3–5 inches) reproduce.

PREVENTION
- Immediate removal of dog waste
- Some heartworm meds prevent roundworm infections
- Prompt de-worming of any infected pup

TREATMENT
- Tablet-form prescription medication

SIGNS OF ROUNDWORMS
- Diarrhea
- Loss of appetite
- Pot-bellied appearance
- Vomiting
- Weight loss

HOW DOGS GET ROUNDWORM
- From eating the feces of infected animals, including dogs, cats, chickens and rodents
- From mother's milk
- From mother's placenta (before birth)
- From eating cockroaches and earthworms

CAN DOGS TRANSMIT THIS TO PEOPLE?
YES. People can get roundworm; however, it is most common in third-world countries.

Notes

76

eparation anxiety

When left alone or separated from their owners, dogs suffering from separation anxiety become extremely anxious and exhibit signs of distress that include vocalizing (barking, howling or whining), destructive behavior, house soiling and refusing to respond to the commands of other caretakers. Dogs with separation anxiety try to remain as close as possible to their owners, following them from room to room and displaying signs of distress when their owner is out of sight.

TIPS TO HELP ALLEVIATE SEPARATION ANXIETY

- **Do not make a big deal about leaving.** If possible, slip out while your dog is occupied. Making a big fuss over him just before you leave will only make him feel your absence more acutely

- **Keep your departure routine to a minimum.** Your dog quickly learns to associate certain behaviors, such as rattling keys and moving at a quicker pace, with your departure

- **Give your dog a Kong toy with a little peanut butter spread inside.** This will keep a dog busy for some time. Saving this and other favorite toys for when you leave may also help to distract him

- **Leave something with your scent on it (a worn t-shirt) for your dog**

- **Play with or exercise your dog before you leave so he will be ready for a nap**

- **When you return, do not greet your dog until he settles down.** (This may take 10 to 15 minutes). Your dog will learn that the faster he calms down, the sooner he will get your attention. Exuberant greetings or any type of punishment for misbehavior upon your return will only heighten your dog's anxiety about future homecomings

> *To improve your relationship with your dog and define your role as the alpha dog, enroll in either group dog obedience classes or private lessons.*

AN ALPHA DOG IS AN ANXIOUS DOG

It may seem incongruous, but the more familiar your dog is with your position as "alpha dog," and his position beneath you, the more secure he will be, both in your presence and in your absence. Following you around so he can watch over you and his turf is classic alpha-dog behavior. Once you teach your dog that you are in charge—that he is not responsible for you and can stay put when you leave a room—he will be more able to calmly accept your departure.

Notes

skunks

TREATMENT

- **Step 1** Examine your dog to make sure he does not have any bites or scrapes. Skunks carry the rabies virus, and if your dog has been bitten, you need to get him to a veterinarian immediately. Do not touch any open wounds

- **Step 2** Flush his eyes with saline solution. Wipe his nose with a sanitary wipe. When your dog gets sprayed by a skunk, the oil often gets in his eyes and stings. In an attempt to stop the burning, your dog will wipe his face against anything he can—including furniture. If your dog exhibits behavior that would indicate that his eyes still sting (after you have flushed them) or if his eyes become overly red or swollen, take him to the vet ASAP!

- **Step 3** Change into clothes you can discard. Skunk spray is an oil, and the odor is almost impossible to get out of fabric

- **Step 4** Treat your dog with a de-skunking formula such as Nature's Miracle Skunk Odor Remover or a home remedy (see below for instructions on how to make a de-skunking mixture). Only treat the part of his body that has been sprayed—treating his whole body will only spread the oil

HOMEMADE DE-SKUNKING MIXTURE

- 1 quart hydrogen peroxide (2 pints standard drugstore-variety 3% hydrogen peroxide)

- 1/4 cup baking soda

- 1 teaspoon liquid dish soap

DIRECTIONS

- Put gloves on before you mix ingredients

- Keep mixture away from your face and your dog's face

- Wet area and work mixture through fur—let set for 3 to 5 minutes

- Rinse thoroughly with water

- Dispose of all unused mixture! (It will explode if kept in a sealed container.)

Important Note: This mixture will bleach your dog's fur.

ticks

See **CRITICAL CONDITIONS**, *page 46.*

a will for your pet?

Do not forget about your pup when you write your will. If you do not make arrangements for your dog, he could wind up in a shelter and be euthanized within days.

YOU SHOULD ADDRESS THE FOLLOWING

- Who will become your dog's guardian if he outlives you

- How much money you're leaving for your dog's care, and what that money should be spent on

- Where your dog's medical records are kept

Be sure to have an attorney confirm that everything has been properly documented.

dog parks

You want your pup's first experience at the dog park to be a positive one. Unless you know that your dog is comfortable interacting with a group of dogs, visit the park during off-peak hours—early mornings on the weekend or mid-morning weekdays—before the dog walkers arrive en masse.

PREP

- Make sure your dog is current on his vaccinations
- Evaluate your dog's socialization skills

PACK

- Water in a re-sealable container for your pup
- Baggies
- Towels to wipe down your muddy pup/ pup's paws
- Ball or Frisbee for fetching

DO NOT BRING

- Treats
- Bones
- Toys
- Anything else that may cause dogs to become possessive

COMMON SENSE CONSIDERATIONS

- Let your dog off leash only once you are inside the designated off-leash area
- Do not keep your dog on leash inside an off-leash dog park. Dogs behave differently when leashed, and unleashed dogs may perceive their behavior to be threatening
- Do not bring your dog to an open (unfenced) off-leash park unless you are certain he is under voice control. Beware of traffic, children and other potential hazards
- Always pick up after your pup. Dog waste spreads worms and other infections between dogs and/or people
- Never assume other people are in control of their dogs—keep a close eye on your dog at all times, especially if he is timid, small or elderly
- Be aware of the particulars of your park, (e.g., amenities, terrain, and environmental hazards like fox tails)
- Be considerate of other park goers (people and dogs) and recognize if you have an aggressive or overly rambunctious dog

> If your dog has any inclination to "play too rough," or fight with other dogs, seek behavioral training. until the issue is resolved, do not put your dog into situations that are likely to bring out aggression.

Notes . . . .

. . . .

. . . .

. . . .

. . . .

dog fights

SIGNS THAT A DOG IS GETTING INTO FIGHT MODE

- Arched back/body
- Ears back
- Growling
- Hair raised
- Tail between his legs

AN OUNCE OF PREVENTION...

It is much easier to prevent a fight before it escalates than to break up a full-blown dog fight. If it seems like your dog is getting ready to attack (or be attacked), gently but firmly grab hold of your dog's collar and pull him away. Loudly and firmly say "no" to the aggressor.

WHAT NOT TO DO

- **Don't put yourself between the dogs or reach in to grab your dog.** Even your own dog is not going to realize that it is you—as opposed to the other dog—he is biting

- **Don't scream.** All hysteria breeds is more hysteria

- **Don't run.** It will incite a chase

WHAT TO DO IF YOU OR YOUR DOG GETS ATTACKED

- Use your water bottle (or a hose if one is handy) to squirt water at the aggressive dog

- If you have pepper or citronella spray—spray the aggressive dog in the face until he stops

- Throw a coat or sweatshirt over the dog to distract him

ONCE THE INCIDENT IS OVER

- Remove your dog from the immediate area—he should remain a safe distance away from the other dog

- If either dog was injured, exchange information with the other owner

- If necessary, call Animal Control

- If necessary, call the police and file a report

Notes

hiking

PREP

- Make sure your dog is current on his flea/tick treatment and vaccinations

- Evaluate your pup's fitness level

- Put together or purchase a pre-packaged first-aid kit (See page 68)

- If your pup has sensitive paws, booties are a must. You do not want your dog to get blisters on his paws. Beyond the obvious pain this would cause, you also need to be mindful of infections

CHECKLIST

- First-aid kit

- Booties/paw protectors

- Water

- High-energy dog snack

Notes . . . .

. . . .

. . . .

. . . .

. . . .

. . . .

. . . .

. . . .

. . . .

hiking hazards

RATTLESNAKES

HOW TO AVOID THEM

- Leash up! Keeping your dog on a leash is the best way to prevent a rattlesnake bite

- Enroll your dog in a rattlesnake-aversion training course where he will learn to avoid the sight, sound and/or smell of a rattle snake through negative association

- Keep an eye out around rocks and crevices

- Do not let your dog dig around under rocks and logs

- Do not walk through tall grass or underbrush

- Do not hike at dusk or dawn, when you are most likely to encounter rattlesnakes

WHAT TO DO IF YOUR DOG IS BITTEN

- If possible, immobilize your dog (activity causes the venom to spread) and carry your dog to the car or arrange for someone to pick up the two of you

- Get your dog to an animal hospital that can administer the anti-venom ASAP

RATTLESNAKE ANTI-VENOM

Not all animal hospitals carry the anti-venom. It is very expensive and has a short shelf life. Be proactive. Find out

- *Which vets in your area carry the anti-venom*
- *How much they keep on hand*
- *How frequently they restock their supply*

excursion tips

When I am in the car I sit . . . .

. . . .

I ☐ **do** ☐ **do not** like riding in the car

If I don't do well in the car, you should . . . .

. . . .

. . . .

> **NEVER LEAVE ME IN THE CAR UNATTENDED!**

I am allowed to play/hike/swim for . . . . . .
minutes/hours

☐ I am likely to chase other dogs

☐ I am likely to chase other animals

Words I know (such as sit, stay or come): . .

. . . .

. . . .

Given the opportunity, I will . . . .

. . . .

. . . .

. . . .

. . . .

nearby places I like to go

Location 1 . . . .

Address . . . .

Cross St. . . . .

City . . . .

Directions . . . .

. . . .

Type of Place . . . .

Beware of (seasonal hazards, etc.) . . . .

. . . .

Avoid (people, dogs, traffic, etc.) . . . .

. . . .

Fenced-in ☐ **Yes** ☐ **No**

I ☐ **am** ☐ **am not** allowed off leash

Stuff to pack . . . .

Best time to go . . . .

> **Notes** . . . .
>
> . . . .
>
> . . . .
>
> . . . .

Location 2 . . . .

Address . . . .

Cross St. . . . .

City . . . .

Directions . . . .

. . . .

Type of Place . . . .

Beware of (seasonal hazards, etc.) . . . .

. . . .

Avoid (people, dogs, traffic, etc.) . . . .

. . . .

Fenced-in ☐ **Yes** ☐ **No**
I ☐ **am** ☐ **am not** allowed off leash

Stuff to pack . . . .

Best time to go . . . .

Location 3 . . . .

Address . . . .

Cross St. . . . .

City . . . .

Directions . . . .

. . . .

Type of Place . . . .

Beware of (seasonal hazards, etc.) . . . .

. . . .

Avoid (people, dogs, traffic, etc.) . . . .

. . . .

Fenced-in ☐ **Yes** ☐ **No**
I ☐ **am** ☐ **am not** allowed off leash

Stuff to pack . . . .

Best time to go . . . .

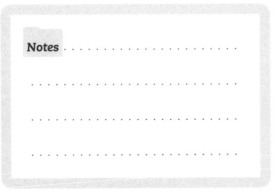

Notes . . . .

. . . .

. . . .

. . . .

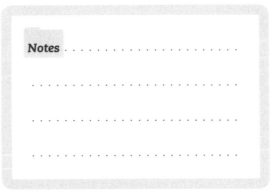

Notes . . . .

. . . .

. . . .

. . . .

Location 4 . . . .

Address . . . .

Cross St. . . . .

City . . . .

Directions . . . .

. . . .

Type of Place . . . .

Beware of (seasonal hazards, etc.) . . . .

. . . .

Avoid (people, dogs, traffic, etc.) . . . .

. . . .

Fenced-in ☐ Yes ☐ No
I ☐ am ☐ am not allowed off leash

Stuff to pack . . . .

Best time to go . . . .

Notes . . . .

. . . .

. . . .

. . . .

. . . .

Location 5 . . . .

Address . . . .

Cross St. . . . .

City . . . .

Directions . . . .

. . . .

Type of Place . . . .

Beware of (seasonal hazards, etc.) . . . .

. . . .

Avoid (people, dogs, traffic, etc.) . . . .

. . . .

Fenced-in ☐ Yes ☐ No
I ☐ am ☐ am not allowed off leash

Stuff to pack . . . .

Best time to go . . . .

Notes . . . .

. . . .

. . . .

. . . .

. . . .

travel preparation

TRAVEL DOS AND DON'TS

DO Confirm that your dog is welcome at your destination

DO Schedule a checkup for your dog and have your vet issue a health certificate and a copy of his vaccination records

DO Trim your pet's toenails so they don't catch on anything, especially if he will be traveling in a crate (See page 75)

DON'T Bring your dog unless he can participate in a majority of your activities. If he's going to be stuck in a hotel room alone, he'll be happier at home

DON'T Bring your dog if he is sick or injured

WHAT TO PACK

- **DOG FOOD** At a minimum, bring enough food for the first 48 hours. Unless you are certain you can get your dog's normal food at your destination, bring enough for the whole trip

- **WATER** Bring a gallon of water from home or purchase filtered water to mix with the water at your destination to help prevent stomach upset. If your dog has a sensitive stomach, you may want to provide your dog with water from home or filtered the entire time

- **BED OR BLANKET** Many of the nicer hotels now provide beds for dogs. However, bringing your dog's bed or blanket from home (with all of its familiar scents) will provide your pup with an added sense of security

- **WATER BOWL** Collapsible and standard

- **FOOD BOWL**

- **SUPPLEMENTS**

- **TREATS**

- **MEDICATIONS**

- **FIRST-AID KIT** (See page 68)

- **TWO TOWELS** to wipe off your dog and protect your car

DO YOU NEED...

- **COLD WEATHER SUPPLIES**
  - Coat
  - Booties

- **WARM WEATHER SUPPLIES**
  - Sun screen
  - Doggles

- **HIKING SUPPLIES** (See page 81)

- **PARK SUPPLIES** (See page 79)

roadtrip tips

- Take your dog out for a stretch and potty break each time you stop for gas
- Always leash up your dog before letting him out of the car
- Park as close to a grassy stretch as possible and watch where your dog steps. (Asphalt gets very hot in the summer)
- Offer your dog water when you stop (most dogs will not drink while the car is moving)
- Never leave your dog in the car unattended, especially in hot or cold weather

> **BY LEAVING YOUR DOG ALONE IN THE CAR, YOU ARE EXPOSING HIM TO THE FOLLOWING RISKS:**
> - **HEAT STROKE IN HOT WEATHER**
> - **HYPOTHERMIA IN COLD WEATHER**
> - **THEFT**

flying tips

- Bring healthy snacks for your dog
- Book a direct nonstop flight
  - during the day in cold weather
  - at night in warm weather
  - during off-peak travel times (avoid holidays and weekends)
- Travel on the same flight as your dog
- Reconfirm your pet's reservation 24 to 48 hours before departure and verify that temperatures are within acceptable ranges for your dog to fly
- Offer your pet food and water within four hours of your arrival at the airport. (Airport officials will have you confirm this in writing at check-in)
- Have the gate attendant confirm that your dog was loaded onto the plane
- Be proactive. If you encounter delays or changes, insist that airline personnel check on your dog
- Carry a current photograph of your pet and a description of the crate (brand, size, color, etc.)

Notes . . . .

. . . .

. . . .

. . . .

. . . .

general airline rules

- You must show proof of vaccinations and present a health certificate issued no more than 10 days prior to your travel date for all legs of the trip. If you will be traveling more than 10 days, review airline policies before making final arrangements

- Your dog must be at least eight weeks old

PETS AS CARRY-ON

Most airlines allow two carry-on pets per coach passenger, and one pet per first-class passenger. However, there is limited space for pets on each flight and space is available on a first come, first served basis.

PETS AS CARGO

Make sure your kennel is airline approved.

- **KENNELS MUST BE**
  - Sturdy
  - Leak-proof
  - Ventilated

- **KENNELS MUST CONTAIN**
  - A hinged or sliding door
  - Grips or handles for lifting
  - A locking device (for kennels with wheels)
  - Two dishes for food and water— accessible from outside the kennel

- **BE SURE TO**
  - Place absorbent bedding—towels, blankets, newspaper—inside the kennel. Do not use colored newspaper. The ink may be toxic to your pet
  - Label the kennel with your pet's name, your contact information and your dog's final destination
  - Attach feeding instructions over a 24-hour period to the kennel
  - Display a **"Live Animals"** label with letters at least one-inch high on the top and on at least one side of the kennel
  - Label the kennel **"This End Up"** on at least two sides

- **YOUR DOG MUST**
  - Be able to stand and sit upright without his head touching the top of the kennel, and be able to turn around and lie down comfortably
  - Not be able to fit any part of his body (nose, paws, tail) through the slats in the kennel

Notes . . . .

. . . .

. . . .

. . . .

. . . .

airline information and pet policies

> *All weight limits include the combined weight of the dog and carrier/kennel.*

Bonus Each dollar spent on pet travel is equivalent to a mile on the One Pass rewards program.

AMERICAN AIRLINES
(800) 433-7300
americanairlines.com

IN-CABIN PET
- **Price** $80 each way
- **Weight limit** 20 pounds
- **Carrier size limit** 23 in x 20 in x 9 in

PET AS CARGO
- **Price** $100 each way
- **Weight limit** 100 pounds
- **Kennel size limit** 40 in x 20 in x 30 in
- **Temperature restrictions** The outside temperature during the trip must be between 45°and 85° (75° for cats and pug-nosed dogs)

CONTINENTAL
(800) 523-3273
Animal Desk (800) 575-3335
continental.com

IN-CABIN PET
- **Price** $80 each way
- **Weight limit** 10 pounds
- **Carrier size limit** 22 in x 14 in x 9 in

PET AS CARGO
- **Price** $99 to $329 each way
- **Weight limit** 150 pounds
- **Kennel size limit** 40 in x 27 in x 30 in
- **Temperature restrictions** None

DELTA
(800) 221-1212
delta.com

IN-CABIN PET
- **Price** $75 each way
- **Weight limit** None
- **Carrier size limit** 17 in x 12 in x 8 in

PET AS CARGO
- **Price** $75 each way
- **Weight limit** 51 pounds
- **Kennel size limit** 48 in x 32 in x 35 in
- **Temperature restrictions** The outside temperature during the trip must be between 45° to 85° (75° for cats and pug-nosed dogs)
- **Blackout Days** May 15 – September 15

JET BLUE
(800) 538-2583
jetblue.com

IN-CABIN PET
- **Price** $50 each way
- **Weight limit** 20 pounds
- **Carrier size limit** 18 in x 15 in x 8 in

PET AS CARGO
Jet Blue does not accept pets as cargo.

NORTHWEST AIRLINES

(800) 225-2525
Pet Center Information Line (888) 692-4738
nwa.com

IN-CABIN PET

- **Price** $80 each way
- **Weight limit** 15 pounds
- **Carrier size limit** 17 in x 12.3 in x 8 in

PET AS CARGO

- **Price** $139 to $299
- **Weight limit** 150 pounds
- **Kennel size limit** 40 in x 27 in x 30 in
- **Temperature restrictions** The outside temperature during the trip must be between 45° and 85° (75° for cats and pug-nosed dogs)
- Blackout days June 1 – September 15

SOUTHWEST AIRLINES

Only service animals are permitted to fly.

U.S. AIRWAYS

(800) 428-4322
usairways.com

IN-CABIN PET

- **Price** $100 each way
- **Weight limit** None
- **Carrier size limit** 21 in x 16 in x 8 in

PET AS CARGO

- **Price** $ 100 each way
- **Weight limit** 100 pounds
- **Kennel size limit** 48 in x 32 in x 35 in

- **Temperature restrictions** The outside temperature during the trip must be between 45° and 85° (75° for cats and pug-nosed dogs)

U.S. Airways does not make reservations for pets as cargo. They operate on a first-come, first-served basis.

UNITED

(800) 864-8331
united.com

IN-CABIN PET

- **Price** $80 each way
- **Weight limit** 20 pounds
- **Carrier size limit** 17 in x 12 in x 8 in

PET AS CARGO

- **Price** $100 to $200 each way
- **Weight limit** 150 pounds
- **Kennel size limit** 40 in x 27 in x 30 in
- **Temperature restrictions** The outside temperature during the trip must be between 45° and 85° (75° for cats and pug-nosed dogs)

car rental agencies

Most car rental agencies allow pets with no additional fee or weight limit, but you will be charged for any damage your dog does to the vehicle. To avoid a cleaning fee, make sure to clean up any pet hair before returning the car.

AVIS
(800) 331-1212
avis.com

BUDGET
(800) 527-0700
buget.com

DOLLAR
Does not allow pets.

ENTERPRISE
(800) 261-7331
enterprise.com

HERTZ
(800) 654-3131
hertz.com

train policies

Amtrak only allows service dogs. Local and commuter train policies vary. Call before travel.

Notes

dog-friendly hotel chains

HOTEL DOS AND DON'TS

DO Keep your dog on a leash at all times while on hotel property

DO Be considerate of other guests and keep your dog at a respectful distance

DO Bring a crate for your dog to sleep in. It is amazing how far a crate and a familiar blanket or bed will go towards easing your pup's anxiety. If you forget the blanket, any article of clothing that has your scent on it will do

DO Put a **Do Not Disturb** sign on the door if you leave your dog in the room alone

DO Make sure your dog has water at all times, especially if you've been flying—dogs get dehydrated too

DO Bring food from home. Many hotels offer a gourmet room-service menu for dogs. But unless your pup regularly dines on tuna tartar or filet mignon, the rich food may upset his stomach

DON'T Leave your pet in the room alone unless you are certain
- You have the hotel's permission to do so
- He won't chew, soil or otherwise destroy the furniture
- He won't bark and disturb other guests

DON'T Assume other guests will like your dog

DON'T Allow your dog to climb on the bed or furniture. If this is impossible to adhere to, bring a sheet or blanket from home to cover the hotel's bedspread and/or furniture.

BEST WESTERN ★★/★★★
800) 428-2627
bestwestern.com
Price Range $$/$$$
Dog Friendly Some locations

COMFORT INN/ COMFORT SUITES ★★
(800) 221-2222
choicehotels.com
Price Range $$
Dog Friendly Some locations

CLARION ★★
(800) 221-2222
clarion.com
Price Range $$
Dog Friendly Charlotte, NC location only

COURTYARD MARRIOTT ★★/★★★
(800) 321-2211
marriott.com
Price Range $$/$$$
Dog Friendly Some locations

DAYS INN ★★
(800) 325-2525
daysinn.com
Price Range $$
Dog Friendly Some locations

DOUBLETREE ★★★
(800) 222-8733
doubletree.hilton.com
Price Range $$$
Dog Friendly Some locations

ECONO LODGE ★
(800) 553-2666
econolodge.com
Price Range $
Dog Friendly Some locations

EMBASSY SUITES ★★★
(800) 362-2779
embassysuites.hilton.com
Price Range $$$
Dog Friendly Some locations

FAIRFIELD INN MARRIOTT ★★
(800) 228-2800
marriott.com
Price Range $$
Dog Friendly Some locations

FOUR SEASONS HOTEL ★★★★★
(800) 545-4000
fourseasons.com
Price Range $$$$$
Dog Friendly Numerous locations

HAMPTON INN ★★
(800) 426-7866
hamptoninn.hilton.com
Price Range $$
Dog Friendly Some locations

HILTON HOTELS ★★★/★★★★★
(800) 445-8667
hilton.com
Price Range $$$/$$$$
Dog Friendly Some locations

HOLIDAY INN ★★
(800) 246-4329
holiday-inn.com
Price Range $$
Dog Friendly Some locations

HOWARD JOHNSON ★/★★
(800) 446-4656
hojo.com
Price Range $/$$
Dog Friendly Numerous locations

INTERCONTINENTAL ★★★★
(888) 303-1758
intercontinental.com
Price Range $$$$
Dog Friendly Some locations

LA QUINTA INN & SUITES ★★/★★★
(866) 725-1661
laquinta.com
Price Range $$/$$$
Dog Friendly Numerous location

MARRIOTT ★★★
(800) 228-9290
marriott.com
Price Range $$$
Dog Friendly Some locations

MOTEL 6 ★
(800) 466-8356
motel6.com
Price Range $
Dog Friendly All locations

QUALITY INN ★★
(800) 221-2222
qualityinn.com
Price Range $$
Dog Friendly Some locations

RAMADA INN ★★
(800) 272-6232
ramada.com
Price Range $$
Dog Friendly Some locations

RENAISSANCE HOTELS AND RESORTS
★★★/★★★★
(800) 468-3571
marriott.com
Price Range $$$/$$$$
Dog Friendly Some locations

RESIDENCE INN MARRIOTT ★★
(800) 331-3131
marriott.com
Price Range $$
Dog Friendly All locations

THE RITZ CARLTON ★★★★/★★★★★
(800) 241-3333
ritzcarlton.com
Price Range $$$$/$$$$$
Dog Friendly Numerous locations

SHERATON HOTELS ★★★
(800) 325-3535
starwoodhotels.com
Price Range $$$
Dog Friendly Some locations

ST. REGIS HOTELS & RESORTS ★★★★★
(877) 787-3447
starwoodhotels.com
Price Range $$$$$
Dog Friendly Some locations

SUPER 8 HOTELS ★
(800) 800-8000
super8.com
Price Range $
Dog Friendly All locations

TOWNPLACE SUITES MARRIOTT ★★
(800) 257-3000
marriott.com
Price Range $$
Dog Friendly Some locations

TRAVELODGE ★
(800) 578-7878
travelodg.com
Price Range $
Dog Friendly Numerous locations

W HOTELS ★★★★
(877) 946-8357
starwoodhotels.com
Price Range $$$$
Dog Friendly Most locations

WESTIN ★★★/★★★★★
(800) 228-3000
starwoodhotels.com
Price Range $$$/$$$$
Dog Friendly Most locations

WYNDHAM HOTELS & RESORTS ★★★/
★★★★
(877) 999-3223
wyndham.com
Price Range $$$/$$$$
Dog Friendly Numerous locations

places to stay

Hotel Name . . . .

☐ Loved it
☐ Want to check it out
☐ It'll do in a bind
☐ Hated it

Address . . . .

Cross St. . . . .

City, State, ZIP . . . .

Phone (. . . .) . . . . — . . . .

Website . . . .

Deposit . . . .

Cleaning Fee . . . .

Weight limit . . . .

☐ Dogs are not allowed in the room alone

Local dog walker/pet sitter

 Name . . . .

 Phone (. . . .) . . . . — . . . . . .

Dog Amenities . . . .

. . . .

. . . .

People Amenities . . . .

. . . .

. . . .

. . . .

Nearby parks/walks . . . .

. . . .

. . . .

. . . .

Nearby attractions . . . .

. . . .

. . . .

. . . .

Notes . . . .

. . . .

. . . .

. . . .

Hotel Name . . . .

☐ Loved it
☐ Want to check it out
☐ It'll do in a bind
☐ Hated it

Address . . . .

Cross St. . . . .

City, State, ZIP . . . .

Phone   (. . . .) . . . . — . . . .

Website . . . .

Deposit . . . .

Cleaning Fee . . . .

Weight limit . . . .

☐ Dogs are not allowed in the room alone

Local dog walker/pet sitter

　　Name . . . .

　　Phone   (. . . .) . . . . . . — . . . . . .

Dog Amenities . . . .

. . . .

. . . .

People Amenities . . . .

. . . .

. . . .

. . . .

Nearby parks/walks . . . .

. . . .

. . . .

. . . .

Nearby attractions . . . .

. . . .

. . . .

. . . .

Notes . . . .

. . . .

. . . .

. . . .

. . . .

Dog Play & Travel | HOTEL LOG

Hotel Name . . . .

☐ Loved it
☐ Want to check it out
☐ It'll do in a bind
☐ Hated it

Address . . . .

Cross St. . . . .

City, State, ZIP . . . .

Phone   (. . . .) . . . . . . — . . . .

Website . . . .

Deposit . . . .

Cleaning Fee . . . .

Weight limit . . . .

☐ Dogs are not allowed in the room alone

Local dog walker/pet sitter

    Name . . . .

    Phone   (. . . .) . . . . . . — . . . .

Dog Amenities . . . .

. . . .

. . . .

People Amenities . . . .

. . . .

. . . .

. . . .

Nearby parks/walks . . . .

. . . .

. . . .

. . . .

Nearby attractions . . . .

. . . .

. . . .

. . . .

Notes . . . .

. . . .

. . . .

. . . .

. . . .

Hotel Name . . . .

　Loved it

　Want to check it out

　It'll do in a bind

　Hated it

Address . . . .

Cross St. . . . .

City, State, ZIP . . . .

Phone 　(　　) 　　 —　　

Website . . . .

Deposit . . . .

Cleaning Fee . . . .

Weight limit . . . .

　Dogs are not allowed in the room alone

Local dog walker/pet sitter

　Name . . . .

　Phone 　(　　) 　　 —　　

Dog Amenities . . . .

. . . .

. . . .

People Amenities

. . . .

. . . .

. . . .

Nearby parks/walks . . . .

. . . .

. . . .

. . . .

Nearby attractions

. . . .

. . . .

Notes . . . .

. . . .

. . . .

. . . .

. . . .

Hotel Name . . . .

☐ Loved it
☐ Want to check it out
☐ It'll do in a bind
☐ Hated it

Address . . . .

Cross St. . . . .

City, State, ZIP . . . .

Phone (. . . .) . . . . . . — . . . .

Website . . . .

Deposit . . . .

Cleaning Fee . . . .

Weight limit . . . .

☐ Dogs are not allowed in the room alone

Local dog walker/pet sitter

    Name . . . .

    Phone (. . . .) . . . . . . — . . . .

Dog Amenities . . . .

. . . .

. . . .

People Amenities . . . .

. . . .

. . . .

. . . .

Nearby parks/walks . . . .

. . . .

. . . .

. . . .

Nearby attractions . . . .

. . . .

. . . .

. . . .

Notes . . . .

. . . .

. . . .

. . . .

. . . .

Hotel Name . . . .

☐ Loved it
☐ Want to check it out
☐ It'll do in a bind
☐ Hated it

Address . . . .

Cross St. . . . .

City, State, ZIP . . . .

Phone   (. . . .) . . . . . . — . . . .

Website . . . .

Deposit . . . .

Cleaning Fee . . . .

Weight limit . . . .

☐ Dogs are not allowed in the room alone

Local dog walker/pet sitter

  Name . . . .

  Phone   (. . . .) . . . . . . — . . . .

Dog Amenities . . . .

. . . .

. . . .

People Amenities . . . .

. . . .

. . . .

. . . .

Nearby parks/walks . . . .

. . . .

. . . .

. . . .

Nearby attractions . . . .

. . . .

. . . .

Notes . . . .

. . . .

. . . .

. . . .

. . . .

Hotel Name ....

   Loved it

   Want to check it out

   It'll do in a bind

   Hated it

Address ....

Cross St. ....

City, State, ZIP ....

Phone ....

Website ....

Deposit ....

Cleaning Fee ....

Weight limit ....

   Dogs are not allowed in the room alone

Local dog walker/pet sitter

   Name ....

   Phone ....

Dog Amenities ....

....

....

People Amenities ....

....

....

....

Nearby parks/walks ....

....

....

....

Nearby attractions ....

....

....

Notes ....

....

....

....

....

Pet Sitter Info Sheet

dog name

Name

Phone

Cell Phone

Work Phone

Destination

Name

Phone

Cell Phone

Work Phone

Destination

VET

Name

Phone

Address

Cross St.

City, State, ZIP

EMERGENCY FACILITY

Name

Phone

Address

Cross St.

City, State, ZIP

EMERGENCY CONTACT

Name

Phone

Cell Phone

I have allergies   Yes   No

My allergies are

If I have an allergic reaction

I am on medication ☐ Yes ☐ No

Medication

Dosage/Frequency

Give with

Medication

Dosage/Frequency

Give with

eating

I eat . . . . . cup(s)/can(s) of . . . .

. . . .

Special preparation . . . .

. . . .

My food is kept . . . .

. . . .

☐ I eat breakfast at . . . .

☐ I eat dinner at . . . .

☐ I eat once a day at . . . .

☐ I do **not** like to be touched while eating

My treats are kept . . . .

☐ I am allowed to have . . . . treats a day

☐ No treats for me—I am
    ☐ on a diet
    ☐ allergic

I ☐ am ☐ am not allowed to eat table scraps

  ☐ Except ☐ Only . . . .

walking

I am usually walked . . . . . times a day
(circle/check all times that apply)

AM	5	6	7	8	9	10	11						
PM	12	1	2	3	4	5	6	7	8	9	10	11	

  ☐ Whenever you wake up
  ☐ After meals
  ☐ After naps
  ☐ Each time you enter the house
  ☐ Before you go to bed

My idea of the perfect walk is
  ☐ A quick potty break
  ☐ A slow stroll
  ☐ A run

My leash is kept . . . .

. . . .

My baggies are kept . . . .

. . . .

attitude

I may have an issue with
  ☐ Big dogs
  ☐ Small dogs
  ☐ All dogs
  ☐ Certain dogs . . . .
  ☐ Visitors
  ☐ Mailmen/delivery men
  ☐ Children
  ☐ Cats
  ☐ Separation anxiety

When backed into a corner, I am more likely to
  ☐ Go down fighting
  ☐ Roll over and play dead
  ☐ Other . . . .

Given the opportunity, I will...
  ☐ Smother you with kisses
  ☐ Bite your finger off
  ☐ Escape
  ☐ Other . . . .

My bark ☐ is ☐ is not worse than my bite

Household chores
  ☐ Mail
  ☐ Plants
  ☐ Trash
  ☐ Blinds/lights
  ☐ Other . . . .

dog name....................

DOG OWNER 1

Name . . . .

Phone (. . . .) . . . . . . — . . . .

Cell Phone (. . . .) . . . . . — . . . .

Work Phone (. . . .) . . . — . . . .

Destination (. . . .) . . . — . . . .

VET

Name . . . .

Phone (. . . .) . . . . . — . . . .

Address . . . .

Cross St. . . . .

City, State, ZIP . . . .

EMERGENCY CONTACT

Name . . . .

Phone (. . . .) . . . . . — . . . .

Cell Phone (. . . .) . . . . — . . . . . .

DOG OWNER 2

Name . . . .

Phone (. . . .) . . . . . . — . . . .

Cell Phone (. . . .) . . . . . — . . . .

Work Phone (. . . .) . . . — . . . .

Destination (. . . .) . . . — . . . .

EMERGENCY FACILITY

Name . . . .

Phone (. . . .) . . . . . — . . . .

Address . . . .

Cross St. . . . .

City, State, ZIP . . . .

I have allergies ☐ Yes ☐ No

My allergies are. . . . .

. . . .

If I have an allergic reaction . . . .

. . . .

I am on medication ☐ Yes ☐ No

Medication . . . .

Dosage/Frequency. . . . .

Give with . . . .

Medication . . . .

Dosage/Frequency. . . . .

Give with . . . .

Pet Sitter Info Sheet

eating

I eat   cup(s)/can(s) of

Special preparation

My food is kept

I eat breakfast at

I eat dinner at

I eat once a day at

I do **not** like to be touched while eating

My treats are kept

I am allowed to have   treats a day

No treats for me—I am
   on a diet
   allergic

I   **am**   **am not** allowed to eat table scraps

   Except   Only

walking

I am usually walked   times a day
(circle/check all times that apply)

AM	5	6	7	8	9	10	11					
PM	12	1	2	3	4	5	6	7	8	9	10	11

Whenever you wake up
After meals
After naps
Each time you enter the house
Before you go to bed

My idea of the perfect walk is
   A quick potty break
   A slow stroll
   A run

My leash is kept

My baggies are kept

attitude

I may have an issue with
   Big dogs
   Small dogs
   All dogs
   Certain dogs
   Visitors
   Mailmen/delivery men
   Children
   Cats
   Separation anxiety

When backed into a corner, I am more likely to
   Go down fighting
   Roll over and play dead
   Other

Given the opportunity, I will...
   Smother you with kisses
   Bite your finger off
   Escape
   Other

My bark   **is**   **is not** worse than my bite

Household chores
   Mail
   Plants
   Trash
   Blinds/lights
   Other

Pet Sitter Info Sheet

dog name . . . .

DOG OWNER 1

Name . . . .

Phone (. . . .) . . . . ——

Cell Phone (. . . .) . . . . ——

Work Phone (. . . .) . . . ——

Destination (. . . .) . . . ——

VET

Name . . . .

Phone (. . . .) . . . ——

Address . . . .

Cross St. . . . .

City, State, ZIP . . . .

EMERGENCY CONTACT

Name . . . .

Phone (. . . .) . . . . . . ——

Cell Phone (. . . .) . . . —— . . . . . .

I am on medication ☐ Yes ☐ No

Medication . . . .

Dosage/Frequency . . . .

Give with . . . .

DOG OWNER 2

Name . . . .

Phone (. . . .) . . . . ——

Cell Phone (. . . .) . . . . ——

Work Phone (. . . .) . . . ——

Destination (. . . .) . . . ——

EMERGENCY FACILITY

Name . . . .

Phone (. . . .) . . . ——

Address . . . .

Cross St. . . . .

City, State, ZIP . . . .

I have allergies ☐ Yes ☐ No

My allergies are . . . .

. . . .

If I have an allergic reaction . . . . .

. . . .

Medication . . . .

Dosage/Frequency . . . .

Give with . . . .

eating

I eat. . . . . cup(s)/can(s) of . . . .

. . . .

Special preparation . . . .

. . . .

My food is kept . . . .

. . . .

☐ I eat breakfast at . . . .

☐ I eat dinner at . . . .

☐ I eat once a day at . . . .

☐ I do **not** like to be touched while eating

My treats are kept . . . .

☐ I am allowed to have . . . . . . treats a day

☐ No treats for me—I am
    ☐ on a diet
    ☐ allergic

I ☐ **am** ☐ **am not** allowed to eat table scraps

   ☐ Except ☐ Only. . . . .

walking

I am usually walked . . . . . times a day
(circle/check all times that apply)

AM	5	6	7	8	9	10	11					
PM	12	1	2	3	4	5	6	7	8	9	10	11

☐ Whenever you wake up
☐ After meals
☐ After naps
☐ Each time you enter the house
☐ Before you go to bed

My idea of the perfect walk is
   ☐ A quick potty break
   ☐ A slow stroll
   ☐ A run

My leash is kept . . . .

. . . .

My baggies are kept . . . .

. . . .

attitude

I may have an issue with
   ☐ Big dogs
   ☐ Small dogs
   ☐ All dogs
   ☐ Certain dogs . . . .
   ☐ Visitors
   ☐ Mailmen/delivery men
   ☐ Children
   ☐ Cats
   ☐ Separation anxiety

When backed into a corner, I am more likely to
   ☐ Go down fighting
   ☐ Roll over and play dead
   ☐ Other. . . . .

Given the opportunity, I will...
   ☐ Smother you with kisses
   ☐ Bite your finger off
   ☐ Escape
   ☐ Other. . . . .

My bark ☐ **is** ☐ **is not** worse than my bite

Household chores
   ☐ Mail
   ☐ Plants
   ☐ Trash
   ☐ Blinds/lights
   ☐ Other. . . . .

dog name ....

DOG OWNER 1

Name . . . .

Phone (. . . .) . . . . . . — . . . .

Cell Phone (. . . .) . . . . . . — . . . .

Work Phone (. . . .) . . . . — . . . .

Destination (. . . .) . . . . — . . . .

VET

Name . . . .

Phone (. . . .) . . . . . . — . . . .

Address . . . .

Cross St. . . . .

City, State, ZIP . . . .

EMERGENCY CONTACT

Name . . . .

Phone (. . . .) . . . . . . — . . . .

Cell Phone (. . . .) . . . . . . — . . . . . .

I am on medication ☐ Yes ☐ No

Medication . . . .

Dosage/Frequency . . . .

Give with . . . .

DOG OWNER 2

Name . . . .

Phone (. . . .) . . . . . . — . . . .

Cell Phone (. . . .) . . . . . . — . . . .

Work Phone (. . . .) . . . . — . . . .

Destination (. . . .) . . . . — . . . .

EMERGENCY FACILITY

Name . . . .

Phone (. . . .) . . . . . . — . . . .

Address . . . .

Cross St. . . . .

City, State, ZIP . . . .

I have allergies ☐ Yes ☐ No

My allergies are . . . .

. . . .

If I have an allergic reaction . . . .

. . . .

Medication . . . .

Dosage/Frequency . . . .

Give with . . . .

eating

I eat . . . . . cup(s)/can(s) of . . . .

. . . .

Special preparation . . . .

. . . .

My food is kept . . . .

. . . .

☐ I eat breakfast at . . . .

☐ I eat dinner at . . . .

☐ I eat once a day at . . . .

☐ I do **not** like to be touched while eating

My treats are kept . . . .

☐ I am allowed to have . . . . treats a day

☐ No treats for me—I am
     ☐ on a diet
     ☐ allergic

I ☐ **am** ☐ **am not** allowed to eat table scraps

  ☐ Except ☐ Only . . . .

walking

I am usually walked . . . . . times a day
(circle/check all times that apply)

AM	5	6	7	8	9	10	11					
PM	12	1	2	3	4	5	6	7	8	9	10	11

☐ Whenever you wake up
☐ After meals
☐ After naps
☐ Each time you enter the house
☐ Before you go to bed

My idea of the perfect walk is
  ☐ A quick potty break
  ☐ A slow stroll
  ☐ A run

My leash is kept . . . .

. . . .

My baggies are kept . . . .

. . . .

attitude

I may have an issue with
  ☐ Big dogs
  ☐ Small dogs
  ☐ All dogs
  ☐ Certain dogs . . . .
  ☐ Visitors
  ☐ Mailmen/delivery men
  ☐ Children
  ☐ Cats
  ☐ Separation anxiety

When backed into a corner, I am more likely to
  ☐ Go down fighting
  ☐ Roll over and play dead
  ☐ Other . . . .

Given the opportunity, I will...
  ☐ Smother you with kisses
  ☐ Bite your finger off
  ☐ Escape
  ☐ Other . . . .

My bark ☐ **is** ☐ **is not** worse than my bite

Household chores
  ☐ Mail
  ☐ Plants
  ☐ Trash
  ☐ Blinds/lights
  ☐ Other . . . .

dog name . . . .

DOG OWNER 1

Name . . . .

Phone   (. . . .) . . . . — . . . .

Cell Phone   (. . . .) . . . . — . . . .

Work Phone   (. . . .) . . . . — . . . .

Destination (. . . .) . . . . — . . . .

VET

Name . . . .

Phone   (. . . .) . . . . — . . . .

Address . . . .

Cross St. . . . .

City, State, ZIP . . . .

EMERGENCY CONTACT

Name . . . .

Phone   (. . . .) . . . . — . . . .

Cell Phone   (. . . .) . . . . — . . . .

I am on medication ☐ Yes ☐ No

Medication . . . .

Dosage/Frequency . . . .

Give with . . . .

DOG OWNER 2

Name . . . .

Phone   (. . . .) . . . . — . . . .

Cell Phone   (. . . .) . . . . — . . . .

Work Phone   (. . . .) . . . . — . . . .

Destination (. . . .) . . . . — . . . .

EMERGENCY FACILITY

Name . . . .

Phone   (. . . .) . . . . — . . . .

Address . . . .

Cross St. . . . .

City, State, ZIP . . . .

I have allergies ☐ Yes ☐ No

My allergies are . . . .

. . . .

If I have an allergic reaction . . . .

. . . .

Medication . . . .

Dosage/Frequency . . . .

Give with . . . .

Pet Sitter Info Sheet

eating

I eat. . . . . cup(s)/can(s) of . . . .

. . . .

Special preparation . . . .

. . . .

My food is kept . . . .

. . . .

- ☐ I eat breakfast at . . . .
- ☐ I eat dinner at . . . .
- ☐ I eat once a day at . . . .
- ☐ I do **not** like to be touched while eating

My treats are kept . . . .

- ☐ I am allowed to have . . . . . . treats a day
- ☐ No treats for me—I am
  - ☐ on a diet
  - ☐ allergic

I ☐ **am** ☐ **am not** allowed to eat table scraps

- ☐ Except ☐ Only . . . .

walking

I am usually walked . . . . . times a day
(circle/check all times that apply)

AM	5	6	7	8	9	10	11						
PM	12	1	2	3	4	5	6	7	8	9	10	11	

- ☐ Whenever you wake up
- ☐ After meals
- ☐ After naps
- ☐ Each time you enter the house
- ☐ Before you go to bed

My idea of the perfect walk is
- ☐ A quick potty break
- ☐ A slow stroll
- ☐ A run

My leash is kept . . . .

. . . .

My baggies are kept . . . .

. . . .

attitude

I may have an issue with
- ☐ Big dogs
- ☐ Small dogs
- ☐ All dogs
- ☐ Certain dogs . . . .
- ☐ Visitors
- ☐ Mailmen/delivery men
- ☐ Children
- ☐ Cats
- ☐ Separation anxiety

When backed into a corner, I am more likely to
- ☐ Go down fighting
- ☐ Roll over and play dead
- ☐ Other . . . .

Given the opportunity, I will...
- ☐ Smother you with kisses
- ☐ Bite your finger off
- ☐ Escape
- ☐ Other . . . .

My bark ☐ **is** ☐ **is not** worse than my bite

Household chores
- ☐ Mail
- ☐ Plants
- ☐ Trash
- ☐ Blinds/lights
- ☐ Other . . . .

Day Care/Boarding Facility Info Sheet

dog name....................

DOG OWNER 1

Name . . . .

Phone   (. . . .) . . . . . . ⎯ . . . .

Cell Phone   (. . . .) . . . . . . ⎯ . . . .

Work Phone (. . . .) . . . . . . ⎯ . . . .

Destination (. . . .) . . . . ⎯ . . . .

DOG OWNER 2

Name . . . .

Phone   (. . . .) . . . . . . ⎯ . . . .

Cell Phone   (. . . .) . . . . . . ⎯ . . . .

Work Phone (. . . .) . . . . . . ⎯ . . . .

Destination (. . . .) . . . . ⎯ . . . .

VET

Name . . . .

Phone   (. . . .) . . . . . . ⎯ . . . .

Address . . . .

Cross St. . . . .

City, State, ZIP . . . .

EMERGENCY FACILITY

Name . . . .

Phone   (. . . .) . . . . . . ⎯ . . . .

Address . . . .

Cross St. . . . .

City, State, ZIP . . . .

EMERGENCY CONTACT

Name . . . .

Phone   (. . . .) . . . . . . ⎯ . . . .

Cell Phone   (. . . .) . . . . . . ⎯ . . . .

I have allergies ☐ Yes ☐ No

My allergies are. . . . .

. . . .

If I have an allergic reaction . . . .

. . . .

I am on medication ☐ Yes ☐ No

Medication . . . .

Dosage/Frequency. . . . .

Give with . . . .

Medication . . . .

Dosage/Frequency. . . . .

Give with . . . .

Day Care/Boarding Facility Info Sheet

eating

☐ I usually eat breakfast at . . . .

☐ I usually eat dinner at . . . .

☐ I only eat one meal a day at . . . .

☐ I am allowed to have . . . . . . treats a day

☐ No treats for me—I am
  ☐ On a diet
  ☐ Allergic

attitude

I may have an issue with

☐ Big dogs
☐ Small dogs
☐ All dogs
☐ Certain dogs . . . .
☐ Separation anxiety

I ascribe to the following philosophy
☐ Share and share alike

☐ What's mine is mine, what's yours
  is yours

☐ What's mine is mine, what's yours
  is mine

☐ What's yours is yours, what's mine
  is yours

I am possessive of
☐ My food
☐ My bed
☐ My toys

When backed into a corner, I am more likely to
☐ Go down fighting
☐ Roll over and play dead
☐ Other . . . .

My bark ☐ is ☐ is not worse than my bite.

Given the opportunity, I will...
☐ Smother you with kisses
☐ Bite your finger off
☐ Escape
☐ Other . . . .

I am ☐ in great physical shape
     ☐ out of shape

I can handle . . . . . . minutes of exercise

Notes

. . . .

. . . .

. . . .

. . . .

. . . .

. . . .

. . . .

Day Care/Boarding Facility Info Sheet

dog name ....

DOG OWNER 1

Name . . . .

Phone (. . . .) . . . . . . — . . . .

Cell Phone (. . . .) . . . . . . — . . . .

Work Phone (. . . .) . . . . . . — . . . . . .

Destination (. . . .) . . . . — . . . .

VET

Name . . . .

Phone (. . . .) . . . . . . — . . . .

Address . . . .

Cross St. . . . .

City, State, ZIP . . . .

EMERGENCY CONTACT

Name . . . .

Phone (. . . .) . . . . . . — . . . .

Cell Phone (. . . .) . . . . . . — . . . .

DOG OWNER 2

Name . . . .

Phone (. . . .) . . . . . . — . . . .

Cell Phone (. . . .) . . . . . . — . . . .

Work Phone (. . . .) . . . . . . — . . . . . .

Destination (. . . .) . . . . — . . . .

EMERGENCY FACILITY

Name . . . .

Phone (. . . .) . . . . . . — . . . .

Address . . . .

Cross St. . . . .

City, State, ZIP . . . .

I have allergies ☐ Yes ☐ No

My allergies are. . . . .

. . . .

If I have an allergic reaction . . . .

. . . .

I am on medication ☐ Yes ☐ No

Medication . . . .

Dosage/Frequency. . . . .

Give with . . . .

Medication . . . .

Dosage/Frequency. . . . .

Give with . . . .

Day Care/Boarding Facility Info Sheet

eating

☐ I usually eat breakfast at . . . .

☐ I usually eat dinner at . . . .

☐ I only eat one meal a day at . . . .

☐ I am allowed to have . . . . . . treats a day

☐ No treats for me—I am
    ☐ On a diet
    ☐ Allergic

attitude

I may have an issue with

☐ Big dogs

☐ Small dogs

☐ All dogs

☐ Certain dogs . . . .

☐ Separation anxiety

I ascribe to the following philosophy
☐ Share and share alike

☐ What's mine is mine, what's yours
   is yours

☐ What's mine is mine, what's yours
   is mine

☐ What's yours is yours, what's mine
   is yours

I am possessive of
☐ My food
☐ My bed
☐ My toys

When backed into a corner, I am more likely to
☐ Go down fighting
☐ Roll over and play dead
☐ Other . . . .

My bark ☐ **is** ☐ **is not** worse than my bite.

Given the opportunity, I will...
☐ Smother you with kisses
☐ Bite your finger off
☐ Escape
☐ Other . . . .

I am ☐ **in great physical shape**
     ☐ **out of shape**

I can handle . . . . . . minutes of exercise

Notes . . . .

. . . .

. . . .

. . . .

. . . .

. . . .

. . . .

. . . .

Day Care/Boarding Facility Info Sheet

dog name . . . .

DOG OWNER 1

Name . . . .

Phone (. . . .) . . . . —

Cell Phone (. . . .) . . . . —

Work Phone (. . . .) . . . . . —

Destination (. . . .) . . . — . . . .

VET

Name . . . .

Phone (. . . .) . . . . —

Address . . . .

Cross St. . . . .

City, State, ZIP . . . .

EMERGENCY CONTACT

Name . . . .

Phone (. . . .) . . . . . . — . . . .

Cell Phone (. . . .) . . . — . . . .

DOG OWNER 2

Name . . . .

Phone (. . . .) . . . . —

Cell Phone (. . . .) . . . . —

Work Phone (. . . .) . . . . . —

Destination (. . . .) . . . — . . . .

EMERGENCY FACILITY

Name . . . .

Phone (. . . .) . . . . —

Address . . . .

Cross St. . . . .

City, State, ZIP . . . .

I have allergies ☐ Yes ☐ No

My allergies are . . . .

. . . .

If I have an allergic reaction . . . .

. . . .

I am on medication ☐ Yes ☐ No

Medication . . . .

Dosage/Frequency . . . .

Give with . . . .

Medication . . . .

Dosage/Frequency . . . .

Give with . . . .

Day Care/Boarding Facility Info Sheet

eating

☐ I usually eat breakfast at . . . .

☐ I usually eat dinner at . . . .

☐ I only eat one meal a day at . . . .

☐ I am allowed to have . . . . . . treats a day

☐ No treats for me—I am
    ☐ On a diet
    ☐ Allergic

attitude

I may have an issue with

☐ Big dogs

☐ Small dogs

☐ All dogs

☐ Certain dogs . . . .

☐ Separation anxiety

I ascribe to the following philosophy

☐ Share and share alike

☐ What's mine is mine, what's yours
    is yours

☐ What's mine is mine, what's yours
    is mine

☐ What's yours is yours, what's mine
    is yours

I am possessive of

☐ My food

☐ My bed

☐ My toys

When backed into a corner, I am more likely to

☐ Go down fighting

☐ Roll over and play dead

☐ Other . . . .

My bark ☐ is ☐ is not worse than my bite.

Given the opportunity, I will...

☐ Smother you with kisses

☐ Bite your finger off

☐ Escape

☐ Other . . . .

I am ☐ in great physical shape
    ☐ out of shape

I can handle . . . . . . minutes of exercise

Notes . . . .

. . . .

. . . .

. . . .

. . . .

. . . .

. . . .

. . . .

Day Care/Boarding Facility Info Sheet

dog name . . . .

DOG OWNER 1

Name . . . .

Phone (. . .) . . . . . — . . . .

Cell Phone (. . .) . . . . — . . . . . .

Work Phone (. . .) . . . . — . . . . .

Destination (. . .) . . . . — . . . . .

VET

Name . . . .

Phone (. . .) . . . . — . . . .

Address . . . .

Cross St. . . . .

City, State, ZIP . . . .

EMERGENCY CONTACT

Name . . . .

Phone (. . .) . . . . . — . . . . . .

Cell Phone (. . .) . . . . — . . . . .

I am on medication ☐ Yes ☐ No

Medication . . . .

Dosage/Frequency . . . .

Give with . . . .

DOG OWNER 2

Name . . . .

Phone (. . .) . . . . . — . . . .

Cell Phone (. . .) . . . . — . . . . . .

Work Phone (. . .) . . . . — . . . . .

Destination (. . .) . . . . — . . . . .

EMERGENCY FACILITY

Name . . . .

Phone (. . .) . . . . — . . . .

Address . . . .

Cross St. . . . .

City, State, ZIP . . . .

I have allergies ☐ Yes ☐ No

My allergies are . . . .

. . . .

If I have an allergic reaction . . . .

. . . .

Medication . . . .

Dosage/Frequency . . . .

Give with . . . .

eating

☐ I usually eat breakfast at . . . .

☐ I usually eat dinner at . . . .

☐ I only eat one meal a day at . . . .

☐ I am allowed to have . . . . . . treats a day

☐ No treats for me—I am
   ☐ On a diet
   ☐ Allergic

attitude

I may have an issue with

☐ Big dogs

☐ Small dogs

☐ All dogs

☐ Certain dogs . . . .

☐ Separation anxiety

I ascribe to the following philosophy

☐ Share and share alike

☐ What's mine is mine, what's yours
  is yours

☐ What's mine is mine, what's yours
  is mine

☐ What's yours is yours, what's mine
  is yours

I am possessive of

☐ My food

☐ My bed

☐ My toys

When backed into a corner, I am more
likely to

☐ Go down fighting

☐ Roll over and play dead

☐ Other . . . .

My bark ☐ **is** ☐ **is not** worse than my bite.

Given the opportunity, I will...

☐ Smother you with kisses

☐ Bite your finger off

☐ Escape

☐ Other . . . .

I am ☐ **in great physical shape**
      ☐ **out of shape**

I can handle . . . . . . minutes of exercise

Notes . . . .

. . . .

. . . .

. . . .

. . . .

. . . .

. . . .

Day Care/Boarding Facility Info Sheet

dog name . . . .

DOG OWNER 1

Name . . . .

Phone (. . . .) . . . . — . . . .

Cell Phone (. . . .) . . . . — . . . .

Work Phone (. . . .) . . . . — . . . .

Destination (. . . .) . . . . — . . . .

VET

Name . . . .

Phone (. . . .) . . . . — . . . .

Address . . . .

Cross St. . . . .

City, State, ZIP . . . .

EMERGENCY CONTACT

Name . . . .

Phone (. . . .) . . . . — . . . .

Cell Phone (. . . .) . . . . — . . . .

DOG OWNER 2

Name . . . .

Phone (. . . .) . . . . — . . . .

Cell Phone (. . . .) . . . . — . . . .

Work Phone (. . . .) . . . . — . . . .

Destination (. . . .) . . . . — . . . .

EMERGENCY FACILITY

Name . . . .

Phone (. . . .) . . . . — . . . .

Address . . . .

Cross St. . . . .

City, State, ZIP . . . .

I have allergies ☐ Yes ☐ No

My allergies are . . . .

. . . .

If I have an allergic reaction . . . .

. . . .

I am on medication ☐ Yes ☐ No

Medication . . . .

Dosage/Frequency . . . .

Give with . . . .

Medication . . . .

Dosage/Frequency . . . .

Give with . . . .

Day Care/Boarding Facility Info Sheet

eating

☐ I usually eat breakfast at . . . .

☐ I usually eat dinner at . . . .

☐ I only eat one meal a day at . . . .

☐ I am allowed to have . . . . . . treats a day

☐ No treats for me—I am
    ☐ On a diet
    ☐ Allergic

attitude

I may have an issue with

☐ Big dogs
☐ Small dogs
☐ All dogs
☐ Certain dogs . . . .
☐ Separation anxiety

I ascribe to the following philosophy
☐ Share and share alike

☐ What's mine is mine, what's yours
   is yours

☐ What's mine is mine, what's yours
   is mine

☐ What's yours is yours, what's mine
   is yours

I am possessive of
☐ My food
☐ My bed
☐ My toys

When backed into a corner, I am more
likely to
☐ Go down fighting
☐ Roll over and play dead
☐ Other . . . .

My bark ☐ **is** ☐ **is not** worse than my bite.

Given the opportunity, I will...
☐ Smother you with kisses
☐ Bite your finger off
☐ Escape
☐ Other . . . .

I am ☐ **in great physical shape**
      ☐ **out of shape**

I can handle . . . . . . minutes of exercise

Notes . . . .

. . . .

. . . .

. . . .

. . . .

. . . .

. . . .

. . . .

Vet Info Sheet

dog name. . . . .

DOG OWNER 1

Name . . . .

Home Phone (. . . .) . . . . . . — . . . . . .

Cell Phone (. . . .) . . . . . . — . . . . . .

Work Phone (. . . .) . . . . . . — . . . . . .

DOG OWNER 2

Name . . . .

Home Phone (. . . .) . . . . . . — . . . . . .

Cell Phone (. . . .) . . . . . . — . . . . . .

Work Phone (. . . .) . . . . . — . . . . . .

PLEASE DON'T FORGET THAT I... (BITE, AM ALLERGIC TO, ETC.) . . . .

. . . .

MY SYMPTOMS INCLUDE

Intermittent/constant . . . . for the last . . . . hours/days/weeks/months

Intermittent/constant . . . . for the last . . . . hours/days/weeks/months

Intermittent/constant . . . . for the last . . . . hours/days/weeks/months

Intermittent/constant . . . . for the last . . . . hours/days/weeks/months

Intermittent/constant . . . . for the last . . . . hours/days/weeks/months

REASONS WHY I MIGHT BE FEELING UNDER THE WEATHER

. . . .

. . . .

. . . .

. . . .

. . . .

Vet Info Sheet

I ☐ **have** ☐ **have not** been eating regularly

I ☐ **have** ☐ **have not** been eliminating regularly

I ☐ **have** ☐ **have not** been sleeping regularly

I ☐ **have** ☐ **have not** been playing regularly

Since I am here anyway, would you also please check

. . . .

. . . .

. . . .

. . . .

Notes . . . .

. . . .

. . . .

. . . .

. . . .

. . . .

. . . .

. . . .

. . . .

. . . .

. . . .

. . . .

. . . .

dog name. . . . .

DOG OWNER 1

Name . . . .

Home Phone (. . . .) . . . . — . . . .

Cell Phone (. . . .) . . . . . . — . . . .

Work Phone (. . . .) . . . . . . — . . . .

DOG OWNER 2

Name . . . .

Home Phone (. . . .) . . . . — . . . .

Cell Phone (. . . .) . . . . . . — . . . .

Work Phone (. . . .) . . . . . . — . . . .

PLEASE DON'T FORGET THAT I... (BITE, AM ALLERGIC TO, ETC.) . . . .

. . . .

MY SYMPTOMS INCLUDE

Intermittent/constant . . . . for the last . . . . hours/days/weeks/months

Intermittent/constant . . . . for the last . . . . hours/days/weeks/months

Intermittent/constant . . . . for the last . . . . hours/days/weeks/months

Intermittent/constant . . . . for the last . . . . hours/days/weeks/months

Intermittent/constant . . . . for the last . . . . hours/days/weeks/months

REASONS WHY I MIGHT BE FEELING UNDER THE WEATHER

. . . .

. . . .

. . . .

. . . .

. . . .

Vet Info Sheet

I ☐ **have** ☐ **have not** been eating regularly

I ☐ **have** ☐ **have not** been eliminating regularly

I ☐ **have** ☐ **have not** been sleeping regularly

I ☐ **have** ☐ **have not** been playing regularly

Since I am here anyway, would you also please check

. . . .

. . . .

. . . .

. . . .

Notes . . . .

. . . .

. . . .

. . . .

. . . .

. . . .

. . . .

. . . .

. . . .

. . . .

. . . .

. . . .

Vet Info Sheet

dog name. . . . .

DOG OWNER 1

Name . . . .

Home Phone (. . . .) . . . . . . —. . . . . . .

Cell Phone (. . . .) . . . . . . —. . . . . . .

Work Phone (. . . .) . . . . . —. . . . . . .

DOG OWNER 2

Name . . . .

Home Phone (. . . .) . . . . . . —. . . . . . .

Cell Phone (. . . .) . . . . . . —. . . . . . .

Work Phone (. . . .) . . . . . —. . . . . . .

PLEASE DON'T FORGET THAT I... (BITE, AM ALLERGIC TO, ETC.) . . . .

. . . .

MY SYMPTOMS INCLUDE

Intermittent/constant . . . . for the last. . . . hours/days/weeks/months

Intermittent/constant . . . . for the last. . . . hours/days/weeks/months

Intermittent/constant . . . . for the last. . . . hours/days/weeks/months

Intermittent/constant . . . . '. . . . for the last. . . . hours/days/weeks/months

Intermittent/constant . . . . for the last. . . . hours/days/weeks/months

REASONS WHY I MIGHT BE FEELING UNDER THE WEATHER

. . . .

. . . .

. . . .

. . . .

. . . .

Vet Info Sheet

I ☐ **have** ☐ **have not** been eating regularly

I ☐ **have** ☐ **have not** been eliminating regularly

I ☐ **have** ☐ **have not** been sleeping regularly

I ☐ **have** ☐ **have not** been playing regularly

Since I am here anyway, would you also please check

. . . .

. . . .

. . . .

. . . .

Notes . . . .

. . . .

. . . .

. . . .

. . . .

. . . .

. . . .

. . . .

. . . .

. . . .

. . . .

Vet Info Sheet

dog name.........................

DOG OWNER 1

Name . . . .

Home Phone (. . .) . . . . . — . . . . . .

Cell Phone   (. . .) . . . . . — . . . . . .

Work Phone (. . .) . . . . . — . . . . . .

DOG OWNER 2

Name . . . .

Home Phone (. . .) . . . . . — . . . . . .

Cell Phone   (. . .) . . . . . — . . . . . .

Work Phone (. . .) . . . . . — . . . . . .

PLEASE DON'T FORGET THAT I... (BITE, AM ALLERGIC TO, ETC.) . . . .

. . . .

MY SYMPTOMS INCLUDE

Intermittent/constant . . . . for the last. . . . hours/days/weeks/months

Intermittent/constant . . . . for the last. . . . hours/days/weeks/months

Intermittent/constant . . . . for the last. . . . hours/days/weeks/months

Intermittent/constant . . . . for the last. . . . hours/days/weeks/months

Intermittent/constant . . . . for the last. . . . hours/days/weeks/months

REASONS WHY I MIGHT BE FEELING UNDER THE WEATHER

. . . .

. . . .

. . . .

. . . .

Vet Info Sheet

I ☐ **have** ☐ **have not** been eating regularly

I ☐ **have** ☐ **have not** been eliminating regularly

I ☐ **have** ☐ **have not** been sleeping regularly

I ☐ **have** ☐ **have not** been playing regularly

Since I am here anyway, would you also please check

. . . .

. . . .

. . . .

. . . .

Notes . . . .

. . . .

. . . .

. . . .

. . . .

. . . .

. . . .

. . . .

. . . .

. . . .

. . . .

. . . .

dog name. . . . .

Name . . . .

Home Phone (. . . .) . . . . . — . . . . . .

Cell Phone (. . . .) . . . . . — . . . . . .

Work Phone (. . . .) . . . . . — . . . . . .

Name . . . .

Home Phone (. . . .) . . . . . — . . . . . .

Cell Phone (. . . .) . . . . . — . . . . . .

Work Phone (. . . .) . . . . . — . . . . . .

. . . .

. . . .

Intermittent/constant . . . . for the last . . . . hours/days/weeks/months

Intermittent/constant . . . . for the last . . . . hours/days/weeks/months

Intermittent/constant . . . . for the last . . . . hours/days/weeks/months

Intermittent/constant . . . . for the last . . . . hours/days/weeks/months

Intermittent/constant . . . . for the last . . . . hours/days/weeks/months

. . . .

. . . .

. . . .

. . . .

. . . .

Vet Info Sheet

I ☐ **have** ☐ **have not** been eating regularly

I ☐ **have** ☐ **have not** been eliminating regularly

I ☐ **have** ☐ **have not** been sleeping regularly

I ☐ **have** ☐ **have not** been playing regularly

Since I am here anyway, would you also please check

. . . .

. . . .

. . . .

. . . .

Notes . . . .

General Dog Service Provider Info Sheet

dog name . . . .

DOG OWNER 1

Name . . . .

Home Phone (. . . .) . . . . — . . . . . .

Cell Phone (. . . .) . . . . — . . . . . .

Work Phone (. . . .) . . . . — . . . . . .

DOG OWNER 2

Name . . . .

Home Phone (. . . .) . . . . — . . . . . .

Cell Phone (. . . .) . . . . — . . . . . .

Work Phone (. . . .) . . . . — . . . . . .

VET

Name . . . .

Phone (. . . .) . . . . — . . . . . .

Address . . . .

Cross St. . . . .

City, State, ZIP . . . .

EMERGENCY FACILITY

Name . . . .

Phone (. . . .) . . . . — . . . . . .

Address . . . .

Cross St. . . . .

City, State, ZIP . . . .

I have allergies ☐ Yes ☐ No

My allergies are . . . .

. . . .

If I have an allergic reaction . . . .

. . . .

. . . .

EMERGENCY CONTACT

Name . . . .

Home Phone (. . . .) . . . . — . . . . . .

Cell Phone (. . . .) . . . . — . . . . . .

I am on medication ☐ Yes ☐ No

Medication . . . .

Dosage/Frequency . . . .

Give with . . . .

Medication . . . .

Dosage/Frequency . . . .

Give with . . . .

General Dog Service Provider Info Sheet

I am seeing you today because . . . .

. . . .

. . . .

. . . .

Given the opportunity, I will
- ☐ Smother you with kisses
- ☐ Bite your finger off
- ☐ Escape
- ☐ Other . . . .

Typically, I am (check all that apply)
- ☐ Anxious in new situations
- ☐ Dog aggressive
- ☐ Easygoing
- ☐ Full of energy all the time
- ☐ Lazy
- ☐ People aggressive
- ☐ Timid
- ☐ Well behaved
- ☐ Other . . . .

. . . .

I am really afraid of . . . .

. . . .

. . . .

I love . . . .

. . . .

. . . .

You should also know . . . .

. . . .

. . . .

Notes . . . .

. . . .

. . . .

. . . .

. . . .

dog name . . . .

DOG OWNER 1

Name . . . .

Home Phone (. . . .) . . . . . — . . . .

Cell Phone (. . . .) . . . . . — . . . .

Work Phone (. . . .) . . . . . — . . . .

DOG OWNER 2

Name . . . .

Home Phone (. . . .) . . . . . — . . . .

Cell Phone (. . . .) . . . . . — . . . .

Work Phone (. . . .) . . . . . — . . . .

VET

Name . . . .

Phone (. . . .) . . . . . — . . . .

Address . . . .

Cross St. . . . .

City, State, ZIP . . . .

EMERGENCY FACILITY

Name . . . .

Phone (. . . .) . . . . . — . . . .

Address . . . .

Cross St. . . . .

City, State, ZIP . . . .

EMERGENCY CONTACT

Name . . . .

Home Phone (. . . .) . . . . . — . . . .

Cell Phone (. . . .) . . . . . — . . . .

I have allergies ☐ Yes ☐ No

My allergies are . . . .

. . . .

If I have an allergic reaction . . . .

. . . .

. . . .

I am on medication ☐ Yes ☐ No

Medication . . . .

Dosage/Frequency . . . .

Give with . . . .

Medication . . . .

Dosage/Frequency . . . .

Give with . . . .

General Dog Service Provider Info Sheet

I am seeing you today because . . . .

. . . .

. . . .

. . . .

Given the opportunity, I will
- ☐ Smother you with kisses
- ☐ Bite your finger off
- ☐ Escape
- ☐ Other . . . .

I am really afraid of . . . .

. . . .

. . . .

Typically, I am (check all that apply)
- ☐ Anxious in new situations
- ☐ Dog aggressive
- ☐ Easygoing
- ☐ Full of energy all the time
- ☐ Lazy
- ☐ People aggressive
- ☐ Timid
- ☐ Well behaved
- ☐ Other . . . .

. . . .

I love . . . .

. . . .

. . . .

You should also know . . . .

. . . .

. . . .

Notes . . . .

. . . .

. . . .

. . . .

. . . .

General Dog Service Provider Info Sheet

dog name . . . .

DOG OWNER 1

Name . . . .

Home Phone (. . . .) . . . . . — . . . . . .

Cell Phone (. . . .) . . . . . — . . . . . .

Work Phone (. . . .) . . . . . — . . . . . .

DOG OWNER 2

Name . . . .

Home Phone (. . . .) . . . . . — . . . . . .

Cell Phone (. . . .) . . . . . — . . . . . .

Work Phone (. . . .) . . . . . — . . . . . .

VET

Name . . . .

Phone (. . . .) . . . . . — . . . . . .

Address . . . .

Cross St. . . . .

City, State, ZIP . . . .

EMERGENCY FACILITY

Name . . . .

Phone (. . . .) . . . . . — . . . . . .

Address . . . .

Cross St. . . . .

City, State, ZIP . . . .

EMERGENCY CONTACT

Name . . . .

Home Phone (. . . .) . . . . . — . . . . . .

Cell Phone (. . . .) . . . . . — . . . . . .

I have allergies ☐ Yes ☐ No

My allergies are . . . .

. . . .

If I have an allergic reaction . . . .

. . . .

. . . .

I am on medication ☐ Yes ☐ No

Medication . . . .

Dosage/Frequency . . . .

Give with . . . .

Medication . . . .

Dosage/Frequency . . . .

Give with . . . .

General Dog Service Provider Info Sheet

I am seeing you today because . . . .

. . . .

. . . .

. . . .

Given the opportunity, I will
- ☐ Smother you with kisses
- ☐ Bite your finger off
- ☐ Escape
- ☐ Other . . . .

Typically, I am (check all that apply)
- ☐ Anxious in new situations
- ☐ Dog aggressive
- ☐ Easygoing
- ☐ Full of energy all the time
- ☐ Lazy
- ☐ People aggressive
- ☐ Timid
- ☐ Well behaved
- ☐ Other . . . .

. . . .

I am really afraid of . . . .

. . . .

. . . .

I love . . . .

. . . .

. . . .

You should also know . . . .

. . . .

. . . .

Notes . . . .

. . . .

. . . .

. . . .

. . . .

dog name . . . .

DOG OWNER 1

Name . . . .

Home Phone (. . . .) — . . . .

Cell Phone (. . . .) — . . . .

Work Phone (. . . .) — . . . .

DOG OWNER 2

Name . . . .

Home Phone (. . . .) — . . . .

Cell Phone (. . . .) — . . . .

Work Phone (. . . .) — . . . .

VET

Name . . . .

Phone (. . . .) — . . . .

Address . . . .

Cross St. . . . .

City, State, ZIP . . . .

EMERGENCY FACILITY

Name . . . .

Phone (. . . .) — . . . .

Address . . . .

Cross St. . . . .

City, State, ZIP . . . .

EMERGENCY CONTACT

Name . . . .

Home Phone (. . . .) — . . . .

Cell Phone (. . . .) — . . . .

I have allergies ☐ Yes ☐ No

My allergies are . . . .

. . . .

If I have an allergic reaction . . . .

. . . .

. . . .

I am on medication ☐ Yes ☐ No

Medication . . . .

Dosage/Frequency . . . .

Give with . . . .

Medication . . . .

Dosage/Frequency . . . .

Give with . . . .

General Dog Service Provider Info Sheet

I am seeing you today because . . . .

. . . .

. . . .

. . . .

Given the opportunity, I will
- ☐ Smother you with kisses
- ☐ Bite your finger off
- ☐ Escape
- ☐ Other . . . .

Typically, I am (check all that apply)
- ☐ Anxious in new situations
- ☐ Dog aggressive
- ☐ Easygoing
- ☐ Full of energy all the time
- ☐ Lazy
- ☐ People aggressive
- ☐ Timid
- ☐ Well behaved
- ☐ Other . . . .

. . . .

I am really afraid of . . . .

. . . .

. . . .

I love . . . .

. . . .

. . . .

You should also know . . . .

. . . .

. . . .

Notes . . . .

. . . .

. . . .

. . . .

. . . .

dog name . . . .

DOG OWNER 1

Name . . . .

Home Phone (. . . .) . . . . — . . . .

Cell Phone (. . . .) . . . . — . . . .

Work Phone (. . . .) . . . . — . . . .

DOG OWNER 2

Name . . . .

Home Phone (. . . .) . . . . — . . . .

Cell Phone (. . . .) . . . . — . . . .

Work Phone (. . . .) . . . . — . . . .

VET

Name . . . .

Phone (. . . .) . . . . — . . . .

Address . . . .

Cross St. . . . .

City, State, ZIP . . . .

EMERGENCY FACILITY

Name . . . .

Phone (. . . .) . . . . — . . . .

Address . . . .

Cross St. . . . .

City, State, ZIP . . . .

EMERGENCY CONTACT

Name . . . .

Home Phone (. . . .) . . . . — . . . .

Cell Phone (. . . .) . . . . — . . . .

I have allergies ☐ Yes ☐ No

My allergies are . . . .

. . . .

If I have an allergic reaction . . . .

. . . .

. . . .

I am on medication ☐ Yes ☐ No

Medication . . . .

Dosage/Frequency . . . .

Give with . . . .

Medication . . . .

Dosage/Frequency . . . .

Give with . . . .

General Dog Service Provider Info Sheet

I am seeing you today because . . . .

. . . .

. . . .

. . . .

Given the opportunity, I will
- ☐ Smother you with kisses
- ☐ Bite your finger off
- ☐ Escape
- ☐ Other . . . .

Typically, I am (check all that apply)
- ☐ Anxious in new situations
- ☐ Dog aggressive
- ☐ Easygoing
- ☐ Full of energy all the time
- ☐ Lazy
- ☐ People aggressive
- ☐ Timid
- ☐ Well behaved
- ☐ Other . . . .

. . . .

I am really afraid of . . . .

. . . .

. . . .

I love . . . .

. . . .

. . . .

You should also know . . . .

. . . .

. . . .

Notes . . . .

. . . .

. . . .

. . . .

. . . .